BLAKE'S VISION

OF

THE BOOK OF JOB

BLAKE'S VISION OF THE BOOK OF JOB

WITH REPRODUCTIONS OF THE ILLUSTRATIONS

A STUDY

BY

JOSEPH H. WICKSTEED

M.A.

LONDON: J. M. DENT & SONS LIMITED
NEW YORK: E. P. DUTTON & CO.
MCMX

"When in Eternity Man converses with Man they enter
Into each others Bosom (which are Universes of delight)."

TO

THE MEMORY OF

My Friend

BENJAMIN KIRKMAN GRAY

Who Showed me first
The Mine concealed in Blake's Prophetic Books
While His Own
Wrath against his Age and Pity for its Children
His Warfare with the World and Peace with Eternity
His Joy in Life as of a Lover and Greeting of Death as a Friend
were themselves the noblest exposition
of Blake's
" Divine-Humanity."

CONTENTS

ON THE REPRODUCTIONS

The reproductions in this book are slightly reduced, the originals being somewhat large for a book intended to be held in the hand and read. They make no pretensions to take the place of Blake's own engravings, which are to be seen in the British Museum and in many private collections. But great pains have been taken to make them a worthy introduction to the study of Blake's poetic designs as used to express the universal ideas he found typified in the incidents of Job's story.

ABBREVIATIONS USED IN REFERRING TO BLAKE'S WORKS AND OTHER AUTHORITIES

Except where otherwise stated, quotations and references in the present work are taken from the originals or from lithographic facsimiles. Blake's spelling and, where at all possible, his punctuation have been followed.

"S. of I."	"Songs of Innocence," engraved 1789.
"Thel"	"The Book of Thel," ,, 1789.
"M. H. H."	"The Marriage of Heaven and Hell," engraved probably 1790 (*vide* Sampson, p. 332).
"America"	"America, a Prophecy," engraved 1793.
"S. of E."	"Songs of Experience," ,, 1794.
"Europe"	"Europe, a Prophecy," ,, 1794.
"Urizen"	"The Book of Urizen," ,, 1794.
"Bk. of Los"	"The Book of Los," ,, 1795.
"Mⁿ."	"Milton, a Poem in two Books,"[1] engraved 1804.
"Jᵐ."	"Jerusalem, The Emanation of the Giant Albion," engraved nominally 1804, but actual date of completion more probably circa 1818 (*vide* Russell, p. 223, note).
"Laocoon"	Sentences engraved by Blake round his plate of the Laocoon statue (Sampson, p. 343, gives date as "circa 1816-20").
"N. N. R. (a)"	Engraved booklet entitled "There is No Natural Religion."
"N. N. R. (b)"	Another engraved booklet with same title; a copy of which is in the possession of the Linnell family. It is correctly transcribed in E. & Y., iii.—spelling, punctuation, etc., being edited—also the "Principles," being numbered First, Second, etc., where Blake uses numerals 1st, 2d, 3d—but 4, 5, 6 —and 7th. (Both these booklets are dated by Sampson (pp. 342, 3) as "probably circa 1790").
"H. C. R. Diary"	"Henry Crabb Robinson's Diary."[2]
"H. C. R. Rem."	" ,, ,, Reminiscences."[2] The MSS. of which are in Dr. Williams's Library (*vide infra* Note on Symons' transcriptions).
"V. L. J."	"A Vision of the Last Judgment" (*vide infra* note 2, p. 19). (Quotations here taken from transcript in Gilchrist, ii.).

[1] On the title-page, as engraved, it appears to be "Milton, a Poem in 12 Books"— but the actual work only contains two books, the last page having "finis" engraved on it. It has been suggested that what appears to be a decimal figure 1 is really only part of the decorative engraving on the page (*vide* Maclagan & Russell's "Milton," A. H. Bullen, Preface, p xiii). In the Brit. Mus. copy this supposed "1" is carefully painted out.

[2] I have to thank Mr. Stephen K. Jones, of Dr. Williams's Library, for kindly checking all my references to the "H. C. R." MSS. and for giving me other help in the proof stage of the work.

"Swed." "Rey."	} Blake's pencil notes in his copies of	Swedenborg's "The Wisdom of Angels concerning Divine Love and Divine Wisdom" Sir Joshua Reynolds' Works	} In the British Museum.
"Lav." Thornton	} Do.	Lavater's "Aphorisms on Man" (Quotations here taken from a careful transcript of the original[1] made by the late Mr John Linnell, Jr.). Thornton's "Lord's Prayer," in the possession of the Linnell family.	
Bacon	Do.	Bacon's Essays (Quotations here taken from Gilchrist).	
Gilchrist		"Life and Works of William Blake," by Alexander Gilchrist, two-volume edition, 1880 (Macmillan).	
Swinburne		"William Blake, a Critical Study," by Algernon Charles Swinburne, 2nd edition, 1868 (Chatto & Windus).	
E. & Y.		"The Works of William Blake, Poetic, Symbolic and Critical," by Edwin John Ellis and William Butler Yeats. 3 vols. Quaritch, 1893.	
Sampson		"The Poetical Works of William Blake. A New and Verbatim text from the Manuscript, Engraved and Letterpress Originals" by John Sampson (Oxford, at Clarendon Press, 1905). All quotations in the present work from poems in the Rossetti or Pickering MSS., and from the "Gates of Paradise" (engraved booklet), are taken from this text.	
Ellis		"The Real Blake, A Portrait Biography," by Edwin J. Ellis (Chatto & Windus, 1907).	
Russell		"The Letters of William Blake, together with His Life, by F. Tatham," edited by A. G. B. Russell (Methuen, 1906) (from which quotations from the letters are here taken).	
Symons		"William Blake," by Arthur Symons[2] (Constable, 1907).	
Illus. 5, 13, etc.		Refers to the commentary in the present work.	
"F.Z." ("Vala")		The unpublished MS. poem presented by Blake to Linnell[3] and	

[1] Mr. Ellis' transcription in his "Real Blake" agrees fairly well with Mr. Linnell's transcription; but the latter follows Blake's characteristic use of capitals, abbreviations and stops, and is probably verbally closer to Blake. It, however, unaccountably omits a most remarkable Note given by Ellis to Aph. 397: "A vision of the Eternal Now" (Ellis, p. 137).

[2] Contains many useful transcripts and reprints of contemporary authorities, including one of the "H. C. R." MSS. (in Dr. Williams's Library), which has, however, various errors, such as "evidences of piety" for "evidences of Christianity," "great admirer" for "quiet admirer," "ordinarily" for "or lunacy," "cruel deity" for "cruel devil," etc., and the incorrect editorial statement that "No earlier reference to him [Blake] occurs in the letter in spite of the sentence which follows." But Gilchrist's extracts of the MS. are incomplete, and E. & Y.'s are from the extremely inaccurate publication edited by the Rev. Thos. Sadler (Macmillan), so that unless we consult the MSS. themselves, we are at present dependent on Mr. Symons' transcript.

[3] E. & Y. i, p. 168.

"F.Z." ("Vala")—*cont.* still in the possession of the Linnell family. It is dated 1797, but was added to at later dates. There has been a rather one-sided controversy between Mr. Ellis and Dr. Sampson as to the proper title for this poem. Messrs. Ellis and Yeats declare (E. & Y. ii. (1893), pp. 295-297) that "Vala" was the third and final title, and the "Four Zoas" the second rejected by Blake. (This Mr. Ellis repeats, in the Chatto & Windus' "Poetical Works" (1906), vol. ii. pp. 229-230). Dr. Sampson, however, has the support of the late owner, Mr. John Linnell, Jr., whose description is to be found in *Sampson* (1905), pp. 337-8. Notwithstanding Mr. Linnell's statement, Mr. Ellis substantially repeats in the Preface to his "Real Blake" (1907), p. ix., his original assertions, but without further evidence.

As, however, Mr. Ellis has considerably modified the original MS. poem in both his versions E. & Y., vol. iii. and Chatto & Windus, vol. ii. (to which latter, references in present work are given), it is convenient to distinguish the MS. as the "Four Zoas," and Mr. Ellis' version as "Vala."

(Readers interested in the question of Mr. Ellis' extensive editing of the MS. will find the matter put from either side as follows: —*Sampson*, General Preface, p. xxviii and p. 351; *Ellis*, "Real Blake," Preface x-xi and chap. vii., especially p. 56. It need only be added here that even from Mr. Ellis' own point of view it is not easy to see why (to take instances from the passage quoted *infra*, p. 12) Blake's "his house, his wife, his children" should be altered to "his wife, his house, his children," or Blake's "While our olive and vine sing and laugh round our door" to "While our olive and wine sing and laugh round our door." These and many similar alterations are not recorded in Mr. Ellis' list of "verbal emendations" E. & Y., iii. pp. 149 *ff.*; Notes, Chatto & Windus, vol. ii. pp. 220 *ff.*)

It is fair to add that Messrs. Ellis and Yeats' "Quaritch" edition of 1893, by the greatly widened area of interest in Blake's work which it created, is probably mainly responsible for a demand, unknown before, for Blake's exact words; a demand which Mr. Ellis has no desire to satisfy.[1]

Other authorities are quoted in full.

---

[1] I have to thank Mr. D. J Sloss of the Liverpool University for sending me transcripts of certain passages in the "Four Zoas" MS., from which I quote—others, such as the great passage on "Experience," I have myself been able to verify from the MS., with the permission of Mr. Herbert Linnell, to whose kindness I am indebted for the opportunity of consulting all the MSS , etc., above referred to as in the possession of the Linnell family.

Experience

(from " Four Zoas " MS.)

" WHAT is the price of experience ?   Do men buy it for a song ?
Or wisdom for a dance in the street ?   No, it is bought with the price
Of all that a man hath, his house, his wife, his children.
Wisdom is sold in the desolate market where none come to buy,
And in the witherd field where the farmer ploughs for bread in vain.
It is an easy thing to triumph in the summer's sun,
And in the vintage ; & to sing on the waggon loaded with corn.
It is an easy thing to talk of patience to the afflicted,
To speak the laws of prudence to the houseless wanderer,
To listen to the hungry raven's cry in the wintry season,
When the red blood is filled with wine and with the marrow of lambs.
It is an easy thing to laugh at wrathful elements,
To hear the dog howl at the wintry door, the ox in the slaughter-house moan ;
To see a god on every wind and a blessing on every blast ;
To hear sounds of love in the thunderstorm that destroys our enemies house ;
To rejoice in the blight that covers his field, & the sickness that cuts off his
    children.
While our olive and vine sing and laugh round our door, and our children bring
    fruits and flowers,
Then the groan and the dolor are quite forgotten, and the slave grinding at
    the mill,
And the captive in chains, and the poor in the prison, and the soldier in the field
When the shattered bone hath laid him groaning among the happier dead.
It is an easy thing to rejoice in the tents of prosperity :
Thus could I sing and thus rejoice : but it is not so with me."

Suffering

(from Conversation)

" Tho' he spoke of his happiness, he spoke of past sufferings, and of suffer-ings as necessary—' There is suffering in Heaven, for where there is the capacity of enjoyment, there is the capacity of pain.' "

Fruition

(from a late MS. Poem)

" I have Mental Joy, & Mental Health,
And Mental Friends, & Mental
    wealth ;
I've a Wife I love, & that loves me ;
I've all But Riches Bodily.

" I am in God's presence night & day,
And he never turns his face away ;
.   .   .   .
Then if for Riches I must not Pray,
God knows, I little of Prayers need say."

BY WAY OF PREFACE

I

The Reading of Blake

It is now several years since, having rashly undertaken to give a popular lecture on " William Blake," I took out the Quaritch "Blake" volumes from a library. My intention was to acquire some elementary knowledge of the mystic writings, principally for the sake of understanding the early poems better. Swinburne of course followed (he should have preceded) and other more recent books and articles. But notwithstanding the help proffered by these various explorers, I confess I could for a long time make little or nothing of the strange works they treated of. Probably most would-be students of Blake have begun with a similar experience.

Yet Blake's prophetic books, with all their apparent formlessness and even monstrosity, exercise from the first a certain nameless spell. Whether their professed interpreters have penetrated to their secret or not, we find it impossible not to believe that they do hold in their unearthly imagery some coherent meaning, and the meaning of the writer of the " Songs of Experience," and of " The Marriage of Heaven and Hell," seems always worth exploring.

It is scarcely too much to say that all who have given serious attention to Blake's great poetic " Prophecies " have found this belief more than confirmed. Waiving moot questions of interpretation aside, students may all agree that the genius which these works reveal (or rather perhaps one must say conceal) is almost of another order of greatness from that of Blake's youth. The flashes of insight, the violent perversity and daring humour, together with his perfect mastery of lyrical form, are now all subordinated to the sustained earnestness of the theme of his great Myth. Blake in his later works appears no longer merely as a brilliant and stimulating eccentric among men of genius, but as one of our great and serious English prophets—how great and serious it is perhaps impossible as yet to form a final estimate. Meanwhile it is certain that his work is a treasury of inspired thinking and beautiful expression, of quite unsurpassed spiritual insight, and withal of a certain pure and childlike wisdom. That he is a supremely virile thinker, I am reluctantly unable to admit, though his ideas prove on examination to have a remarkable and unexpected consistency of their own, while there perhaps never was a thinker more suggestive and liberating. Often abysmally unintelligible as he still is, even to the student, he is seldom or never without inherent force and nobility when understood. And the fact that he was weak where the great age that followed him was strong, is more than compensated for by the fact that he did his thinking in regions where the main current of nineteenth-century thought never went at all. As a consequence of this sustained independence of mental life, Blake's anticipations in his later work of philosophic and ethical ideas that we almost regard as characteristically twentieth century, are scarcely less striking than his alleged poetic anticipations of the great singers of last century.[1]

---

[1] It is no doubt easy to over-estimate the importance of Blake's points of contact with either Nietzsche on the one hand or Tolstoi on the other (*vide* Illus. 3, 18, 20, etc.); or again with such men as William James, Bernard Shaw or R. J. Campbell. The possibility of finding such parallels, however, shows that, even as a thinker, Blake has something of the perennial youth of genius, while the wealth of his poetic imagination often invests his conceptions with a worth entirely their own.

But this growth of strength and dignity in his later work was achieved, it seems, at the price of finally surrendering all hope of being heard by his own age. Having vainly stormed the eyes and ears of his public for more than half his working life, he seems at last to care only for the pure expression of his best and deepest in a medium which proved intelligible only to himself. It became his ambition now "to be a memento in time to come and to speak to future generations by a sublime allegory," and "allegory," he says, "addressed to the intellectual powers, while it is altogether hidden from the corporeal understanding, is my definition of the most sublime poetry." [1]

From these depths of obscurity both of text and design, Blake only very partially emerges in the illustrations which are the subject of the present study. When first searching for clues to the meaning of Blake's designs in general, my attention was attracted to the Job inventions by noticing that some of the figures in them were modified repetitions of earlier ones in the prophetic books, and this gave a momentary hope that their use as illustrations of a generally intelligible work like the Book of Job, might throw light upon their meaning in Blake's own dark writings.

This did not prove to be the case. But once the Job designs had been closely scrutinised, it became evident that they were not *mere* illustrations of the Book of Job. They certainly contained some peculiarly Blakean point of view, which if only it could be deciphered, must be of especial interest, as the expression of his last years.

This conviction that the designs themselves were something other than literal illustrations, was more than confirmed by a fuller knowledge of Blake's mind. Indeed it became continually more astonishing that Blake of all men should have become the

[1] Letter to Thomas Butts, 6th July 1803 (Russell, p. 121).

illustrator of the Book of Job.   And in point of fact his work is one of those great moments in creative art when the clash of con-trasted genius produces not neutrality, but something unexpectedly great and new.

The story of Job, both in its amazing modernness of thought and its ancient form or setting, is in striking contrast to all Blake's most cherished beliefs.   The unknown genius who wrote the original poem daringly presents the mystery of evil as humanly insoluble ; and his inscrutable Deity is enshrined in the marvels of external nature.   Again the book in its present form contains the archaic idea of atonement by burnt-offering, and a largely material conception of adversity and restored prosperity.   It would be scarcely possible to choose four ideas more antipathetic to Blake's philosophy than these.   And when we add that it is extremely doubtful how far he conceived Job's proverbial " patience " as being a virtue at all, we see how hard it is to find the point of contact.

But if there was no natural and obvious point of contact, Blake was to be trusted to find or devise one.

He had been inspired and even haunted by Job's story for some thirty years before he undertook the present engravings.[1] He must re-read it in the light of spiritual vision.   And with the

---

[1] In 1796 (?) he made a sketch in Indian ink of Job and his Friends from the text : " What is man that Thou shouldst . . . try him every moment ? " Job vii. 17, 18 (Gilchrist, ii. p. 256). In the Carfax Exhibition (1906) was shown a coloured engraving of the same subject, described as " Painted and engraved by William Blake, 1793 " (Catalogue, p. 18, *cp.* Gilchrist, vol. i. p. 133).   There is an undated water-colour of Job confessing his presumption, quite unlike any of the designs in the present series (Gilchrist, ii. p. 236).   And there is an undated " fresco," or painting, in tempera of Satan tormenting Job, closely similar to the sixth illustration in the present series. This does not include the complete series of paintings from which the present series of engravings and another of paintings was taken (Gilchrist, ii. pp. 223-225).   There are replicas of some of these (Gilchrist, ii. 226, etc.).

courage of genius it is the very features in the book where he most sharply differs from its point of view which he chiefly selects to treat.

The solution begins to unfold itself when we consider Blake's method of illustrating other works. Certain of his designs to his own "Songs of Innocence" represent something apparently quite remote from the ostensible subject of the song. They contain, in fact, suggestions of wider, underlying ideas, out of which the poem seems to spring like the flower from its tree.[1] The "Blair's Grave" designs, again, have scarcely anything to do with the morbid and didactic poem they are bound up with, and seem rather an attempt to lift the subject on to a higher plane; an end which they certainly attain.

But fortunately we have a word from Blake's own lips, which tells us something of his ideas as to the functions of an illustrator. It was during his last years, when at work upon these designs, that Crabb Robinson, the diarist, became acquainted with him. And in one of his recorded conversations with him, Blake quaintly remarks that Milton (in the spirit) had recently come "to ask a favour" of him. "He said he had committed an error in his Paradise Lost, which he wanted me to correct, in a poem *or picture*; but I declined I said I had my own duties to perform."[2]

It is important to notice that though Blake declines the honour, it is not from any sense of its being intrinsically inappropriate. It may be that he thought he had already done his duty by Milton. For, in his illustrations to "Paradise Lost," he more than

[1] Note especially "The Blossom" and also "The Divine Image," "S. of I." In these designs the forked and lambent growths may probably symbolise the "divine essence" (for treatment of which subject, *vide infra* Illus. 17).

[2] "H. C. R. Rem.," 1825 (Symons, pp. 295-6; italics mine).

B

once gives the story an inspired turn that might almost be said to "correct" the poem.[1] But, in any case, the Miltonic vision found him at the moment engaged in an act of piety towards a still greater spirit, and in the present work we shall find Blake sparing no pains to give a rendering of the Job story in harmony with what were to him the essential truths of life.

I must now turn for a moment to my chance discovery of the clue. I noticed, what has probably often been noticed before, that Job and his Deity are characteristically represented with different feet similarly posed, the former showing his left, where the latter shows his right. This apparently trivial fact suggested that Blake definitely intended to show a correspondence between the two figures, and that the somewhat disconcerting likeness between the man and his God was no accident ; the two personifications representing different aspects of the same being. There are unmistakable indications that Satan, too, is an aspect of Job's own soul—a "state" as Blake would call it. And he says : "Men are born with an Angel and a Devil."[2] Jehovah is the angel, as indicated by the text in the second illustration, where he is described as the "Angel of the Divine Presence." "Every man has a Devil in himself," Blake says, "and the conflict

---

[1] The greatest example of this is in his illustration to the passage where God, the Son, offers to descend and save man. The passionate gratitude expressed in the Father's attitude, makes it seem that it is He himself whom the Son is redeeming. This was, no doubt, what Blake meant by the illustration. The other conspicuous instance is less significant, though scarcely less characteristic. It is where the chariot, in which God the Son rides forth to drive out the rebel host, is represented simply as a glowing sun, from the heart of which the Son stretches forth His bow against the Satanic host (Gilchrist, ii. p. 219; *vide* reproduction in Liverpool Booksellers' "Paradise Lost"; *cp.* Milton's "Paradise Lost," Book vi. ll. 750*ff.*).

[2] "H. C. R. Rem.," 7th Dec. 1826 (Symons, p. 304) ; *cp.* "H. C. R. Diary" (Symons, p. 270).

between his *Self* and God is perpetually carrying on."[1] The whole Job drama, as set forth in Blake's illustrations, appeared then most likely to be the story of a primarily subjective experience; the account of a man's inward struggle and triumph; the conflict between his indwelling Good, and Evil, powers. This at least was a truly Blakean conception, and if it proved true, seemed likely to throw a flood of light upon this, and incidentally upon all, Blake's work. The idea once started was soon corroborated by such facts as that in the ninth illustration, where Eliphaz is speaking of *his* vision of God, the Deity bears the same kind of facial likeness to the speaker as he does elsewhere to Job. And that such details as these were not mere accidents is attested by Blake himself in a possibly contemporary[2] document descriptive

[1] "H. C. R. Rem.," 19th Feb. 1826 (Symons, p. 303, incorrectly given as "perpetually going on"; *cp.* "H. C. R. Diary," Symons, p. 268).

[2] "A Vision of the Last Judgment" (from the Rossetti MS.). This important essay on a picture of the Last Judgment does not describe any of the several known examples of the subject, but may be supposed (Russell, note on pp. 198 and 199) to refer to the large lost picture, 1820 to 1827 (Gilchrist, ii. p. 223), and still being worked upon at the end of Blake's life (Gilchrist, i. pp. 262 and 401). The difficulty of dating this essay so late is that it occurs in the MS. book (Sampson, "Rossetti" MS., p. 138 *ff.*), the last dated entry of which is 4th Aug. 1811 (Sampson, p. 146). But it is clearly a late entry, as it is one of those described by Sampson as "scattered here and there throughout the book with frequent encroachments upon the sketches" (Sampson, p. 140). A difficulty remains in the heading, which occurs on the third of the pages containing these fragments (Sampson, p. 147), "For the year 1810. Addition to Blake's Catalogue of Pictures, etc." The account, therefore, seems to have been *begun* long before the picture it is supposed to describe. In the absence of clearer evidence on the matter, I hazard the suggestion, with due reserve, that Blake, being too poor during this period to get materials to begin painting the great work with which his mind was full, sought relief in filling up his old note-book with the dissertation, which was almost certainly added to when the picture was more or less complete. At all events, 1820 (Symons, p. 229; Gilchrist, ii. p. 223, says "circa 1822") is the date when the first series of Job illustrations was completed for Butts, so that one can safely say that Blake's conceptions, both of the Book of Job and of the Last Judgment, were growing to a final form in his mind during the decade 1810-20, and,

of another of his works, where he says : "I entreat, then, that the spectator will attend to the hands and feet ; to the lineaments of the countenance : they are all descriptive of character, and not a line is drawn without intention, and that most discriminate and particular." [1]

Careful comparison of Blake's designs and texts at last completely confirmed the symbolical device in which he here hides his profound conceptions of man's inward and outward being ; his spiritual and bodily life. A master-key had been found which proved to explain not only Blake's symbolical use of the hands and feet, and of the right and left sides, but unveiled a great spiritual theme, running through and unifying the whole Job series, and giving a characteristic rendering of the story, such as afforded an invaluable revelation of Blake's final and maturest thought. [2]

As was to be expected, a further result of investigations, begun primarily to verify this clue, was that many points besides those interpreted by it began to explain themselves in the light of passages in Blake's writings. Perhaps the most important of these

that the remaining years of his life were mainly devoted to working them out. This accounts for the immense interpretative value of the Last Judgment essay in many of the crucial problems of the Job Together with the Crabb Robinson conversations (which are contemporary with the actual engraving of the plates) and the great treasure-house of the "Jerusalem" (also probably completed during the decade 1810-20, viz, 1818, Russell, p. 223, note), to which must perhaps be added the Laocoon (circa 1816-1820, Sampson, p. 343), it forms the dictionary and grammar for the reading of the Job. It must, however, be added that these works themselves require to be read in the light of Blake's early work (especially "Songs of Experience," "Marriage of H. and H ," "There is No Natural Religion," pencil notes to "Swedenborg" and "Lavater," etc.). We must find the relation of such late sayings as "What is Mortality but the things relating to the Body, which Dies ?" ("J^{m}.", p. 77), with such early ones as that "Energy is the only life and is from the Body" ("M. H. H.," p. 4), if we are to read aright Blake's final message in the Job (vide Illus. 12).

[1] Gilchrist, ii. p. 193.   [2] Vide Appendix A.

was the discovery as to what was represented by the two figures descending in Satan's flame on either side of himself, when he is finally hurled into the abyss. Messrs. Ellis and Yeats describe them as " Sin and Death," [1] and in the classical description in Gilchrist's " Life," they might almost be inferred to be " Hell and Destruction," which are referred to in the marginal text. [2] But in my opinion there can be no doubt that Blake intended them to represent the evil selves or aspects of Job and his wife, which first appear as shades in Satan's flame in Illustration 2, but have at last been given " a body " that they " may be cast off for ever " [3]—the idea that evil must be embodied and made concrete or " experienced " before it can be escaped and rejected, being one which recurs in some form at every stage of Blake's thought. [4]

[1] E. & Y. vol. i. p. 134, where they are described as "two female figures," on what grounds I do not know.

[2] Gilchrist, i. p. 332.

[3] " J^m.", p. 12, l. 13.

[4] Examples from works of several different periods will suffice to prove this. (1) In the " Marriage " we get the idea in its cruder form: " The road of excess leads to the palace of wisdom," " If the fool would persist in his folly he would become wise" (" M. H. H.," p. 7). (2) In a proposed motto for the " Songs of Innocence and of Experience" (Sampson, p. 175), Blake describes Experience as a process of sifting good and evil, which seems to anticipate in a more fanciful form the *fixing systems to deliver individuals*, of Jerusalem ; " Till Experience teaches them to *catch and to cage* the Fairies and Elves" (italics mine), by which process good and evil are at last distinguished, " And the Eagle is known from the Owl." (3) In the " Four Zoas " MS. the idea is more developed : " All mortal things made permanent that they may be put off" (*cp.* " Vala," viii. 475). (4) In " Jerusalem " it appears to be mainly intellectual, and consists in " making states permanent " and in " fixing systems " to " deliver individuals" from those states and systems (ref., " J^m.", p. 9, ll. 29, 30; p. 11, l. 5; p. 12, ll. 12-13; p. 25, l. 13; p. 55, l. 65; p. 90, l. 38).

It is here part of the work of redemption to compel false systems to become explicit. " Giving a body to Falsehood, that it may be cast off for ever" (" J^m.", p. 12, l. 13). " That he who will not defend Truth, may be compelld to defend a Lie " (" J^m.", p. 9, ll. 29-30 ; *cp.* " M^n.", p. 6, ll. 47-48). Or in one of those still more whimsical Blakean utterances : " Go thou to Skofield : ask him if he is Bath or if he is

The significance of the diurnal motion in the scheme of this work was first suggested to me by Messrs. Ellis and Yeats' system of Blake interpretation ; though they do not seem, in their interesting account of the Job illustrations, to have realised the bearing of their discovery here.[1]

The further substantiation of this feature of their system, and of my own discovery of the right-and-left symbolism, will be found

---

Canterbury. Tell him to be no more dubious : demand explicit words " (" J^m.", p. 17, ll. 59-60). And an interesting passage on p. 49 of "J^m.", concludes (ll. 70, 71) :

> " Because the Evil is Created into a State, that Men
> May be deliverd time after time evermore. Amen."

The idea is also quite explicit, though in a somewhat different form, in such a passage as "J^m.", p. 90, ll. 35-38 ; which explains the nature of the Redemption as conceived by Blake :—

> " . . . by his Maternal Birth he is that Evil-One
> And his Maternal Humanity must be put off Eternally
> Lest the Sexual Generation swallow up Regeneration
> Come Lord Jesus take on thee the Satanic Body of Holiness."

(5) In the " Vision of Last Judgment " (*vide supra* note 2, p. 19) the idea is explicit enough, even for our " corporeal " understanding. " No man can embrace true art till he has explored and cast out false art (such is the nature of mortal things) " (Gilchrist, ii. p. 195).

It ought, perhaps, to be added that when Blake talks in " Jerusalem " of " making permanent " and " fixing," or even " giving a body to," he may mean intellectualising rather than corporealising (*cp.* "J^m.", p. 92, ll. 15-20). This, however, is a very complex question, and is irrelevant to the present point, which is that evil must be, in some sense, actively realised before it can be ejected.

[1] E. & Y., i. pp. 130-135. The value of Messrs. Ellis and Yeats' general system of Blake interpretation has been estimated, not very favourably, by Dr. Sampson on p. 328 of his book. Mr. Ellis himself shows that he is keenly alive to the difficulties and dangers besetting the worker in this field, in five lines which occur at the head of page 238 in his second volume of the Chatto & Windus' " Poetical Works." The incompleteness of their references both to Blake's own works and to the sources from which they derive his ideas, makes it very difficult to test their work. Alternative or supplementary systems have been promised by other students for some years.

in appendices at the end of the volume. Apart from these two fundamental ideas underlying the whole series, I have endeavoured to base my interpretation strictly upon Blake's more explicit and unveiled utterances, and, as far as possible, my references are to passages which the general reader can understand and appreciate without the aid of a special code of interpretation. Such passages are numerous and beautiful, though somewhat scattered throughout Blake's darker utterances; and, moreover, it is upon such explicit sayings that all interpretation must ultimately depend. In order to carry out this plan, I have been obliged frequently to omit words and phrases that belong to Blake's esoteric language, and which seemed likely to interrupt or confuse the meaning for the general reader. Such lacunæ are always indicated by dots, and the exact references will enable students to satisfy themselves that in taking this liberty I have taken pains not to do violence to Blake's true intention.

Although there is an acknowledged fascination in all attempts at puzzle-solving, it must not be supposed that any considerable portion of the interest of the Job illustrations lies in the opportunity they afford for this amusement.

Blake was burning with a great message which he could not leave unuttered, even though he found his contemporaries almost entirely unready for it. He seems, therefore, to have deliberately chosen to hide it in a precious casket, even at the risk of this remaining for ever locked.[1]

To realise it in its fulness, as uttered in the Job illustrations, students should go to the original engravings and use the following notes, as a mountaineer uses map and compass to guide him into

[1] *Vide supra*, p. 15.

the presences of the mountain heights.   But even through the
means of reproductions and of such word-translations as have been
here attempted, something, it is hoped, may be learnt of the price-
less beauty of which the mind of this great and lonely thinker was
full.

Blake's dominant theme in all his later work is the reconciliation of the individual life with the universal life of humanity
(Christ) :[1] and the re-discovery in that reconciliation of a lost God
and Heaven.[2]   Under the form of Job's misfortunes and subsequent restoration to prosperity, Blake treats the burning problem,
alike of religion, politics and art.[3]   Reconciliation of the
individual's unfettered liberty with the solidarity of Society ;
reconciliation of the soul's experience with the Church's historic

[1] "Jesus . . . the Lord the Universal Humanity" ("J^m.", p. 96, ll. 3 and 5, etc., etc.)
[2] *Cp.* The opening lines of "Jerusalem," chap. i.

> " This theme calls me in sleep night after night, & ev'ry morn
> Awakes me at sun-rise, then I see the Saviour over me
> Spreading his beams of love, & dictating the words of this mild song.
> Awake ! awake O sleeper of the land of shadows, wake ! expand !
> I am in you and you in me, mutual in love divine :
> Fibres of love from man to man thro Albions pleasant land.
>
> .   .   .   .
>
> Where hast thou hidden thy Emanation lovely Jerusalem
> From the vision and fruition of the Holy-one ?
> I am not a God afar off, I am a brother and friend ;
> Within your bosoms I reside, and you reside in me :
> Lo ! we are One ; forgiving all Evil ; Not seeking recompense,
> Ye are my members O ye sleepers of Beulah, land of shades ! "

("J^m.", p. 4, ll. 3-21.)

[3] Which were to him essentially the same :—

> "What is a Church ? & What
> Is a Theatre ?   Are they Two & not One ? can they Exist Separate ?
> Are not Religion & Politics the Same Thing ?   Brotherhood is Religion."

("J^m.", p. 57, ll. 8-10.)

atmosphere and institutions; reconciliation of the integrity of artistic inspiration with popular expression; these are questions of which we become ever more conscious with the advance and growing complexity of civilisation. And Blake, though not dealing with the questions precisely in these forms, has a profound if childlike solution for this whole class of difficulties.

On the one hand his individualism is uncompromising and ultimate. All good (and evil too—but evil is to him only a negation[1]), is inward and individual good; it is good to me, or you, or some other particular person or creature.[2] Salvation, happiness, beauty, and in a certain ultimate sense God, are brought to being in, and only in, the individual soul. On the other hand, the individual, however noble, heroic or successful in himself, is the mere incarnation of Satan until he has lost and re-discovered

[1] "He allowed, indeed, that there is error, mistake, etc., and if these be evil—then there is evil, but these are only negations." "H. C. R. Diary," 17th Dec. 1825 (Symons, p. 262).

[2] The most explicit statement of this is in a passage from the "Last Judgment" MS., which Ellis and Yeats say Blake drew his pen through—though, as they remark, it does not follow that he withdrew his assent thereto. "There is not an error but has a man for its agent; that is, it is a man. There is not a truth but it has also a man. Good and evil are qualities in every man, whether a good or evil man" (E. & Y. i. p. 232). But the idea is implicit in such a passage as the following from the "Proverbs of Hell" ("M. H. H.," p. 9). "Prayers plow not! Praises reap not! Joys laugh not! Sorrows weep not!" (cp. ib.: "As the plow follows words, so God rewards prayers"). Without the personal will and realisation of things, nothing happens—there is neither hope nor love, good nor grief. Cp. also

"He, who would do good to another, must do it in Minute Particulars General Good is the plea of the scoundrel hypocrite & flatterer:"
("J^m.", p. 55, ll. 60-61.)

"But General Forms have their vitality in Particulars: & every Particular is a Man:" ("J^m.", p. 91, ll. 29-30.)

his own life in the Divine-humanity; in *Christ* and his bride *Jerusalem*; that is in *Man* as he is to be found in actual *men*.[1]

In conclusion, I would like if possible to conciliate in advance two types of adverse criticism for which I have considerable sympathy. In so far as my exposition of Blake's meaning in these illustrations is really new, there will inevitably be some of his old admirers to whom not only my method, with its intrinsic defects, but my conclusions themselves are antipathetic and therefore unconvincing. To these I would urge the fact that every great genius requires to be approached many times, and from many sides, before the whole worth of his art can be known. And so long as interpretation is based on genuine investigation of the works themselves, it cannot fail, even if mistaken, to further the ultimate knowledge of the truth.

Again, there are doubtless still many of Blake's admirers who think it a mistake to take him quite seriously at all. The crude charge of insanity which used to be so lightly levelled against him is surely almost dead. But there remains a too well-founded charge of waywardness and extravagance, such as cannot be attributed to normal processes of mind even in the blast furnace of genius. It is an easy escape from the labour of interpretation to attribute every thing not understood to disease of mind. Thanks to the devoted labours of a few Blake students, such an attitude has for some time past been inadmissible.[2]   But there

---

[1] These points will be found dealt with in the Introduction and Illustrations, especially Illus. 2, 10, 17 and 18.

[2] It seems inevitable that this charge of insanity should be both periodically revived and indignantly denied. For Blake's undoubtedly abnormal mentality was controlled by a not less remarkable faculty for artistic and even philosophic unity and coherence. In one sense he was further removed from the lunatic than those who have less cerebral peculiarity. And even if there were real lapses of control, these were rather literary than practical. His actual life seems to have been conspicuous for its sanity.

seems much more justification for those who urge that his designs and lyric poems are so good unexplained that it is unwise to attempt to explain them.

In reply to this attitude I would urge two points in defence of the present study. In the first place it must be remembered that of his two best-known works, the "Songs of Innocence" and the Job designs, the former was published when he was thirty-two and the latter when he was sixty-eight. It seems obvious then that we must pay some attention to the work of his middle years, if we are to really understand this last. This makes it quite impossible to refrain entirely from trespassing on the field of interpretation of the mystic and mythological system ; for the works of his middle years are all upon this theme. Interpretation of other works, however, has only been introduced into this study where questions concerning the interpretation of the Job illustrations were directly involved.

The defence of the interpretation of these illustrations themselves is somewhat different. It is true that without any explanation they have a strength and beauty which has always commanded the admiration of a select public. But probably every Blake-lover will admit that the haunting power of all his designs is due to something not actually on the paper. They awake ideas ; sometimes purely sensational, sometimes emotional or intellectual, but always as important to our enjoyment as the actual outlines, or things portrayed. Indeed the purely decorative beauty, though often very great, is seldom without some accompanying crudity or extravagance that threatens seriously to detract from our enjoyment. It is radiant light, rushing motion, ponderous weight, and like impalpable things, that seem from the first the distinguishing features of his work. But he is also able to show inward emotions

with unique power. Fear, desolation, rapture, love are inherent in
his compositions. To miss these is to see the outward shapes
without the inner life that makes them instinct with beauty or
strength. And in the same way, Blake's profound conceptions of
human life and poetic vision are the soul of his Job designs. As
mere engravings we may admire them as we admire a statue ; but
to understand what they tell us of his deeper thought is to see that
statue, not indeed wrought into a perfect work of art, but literally
turned to life.

II

NOTE ON BLAKE'S LIFE

For the benefit of those to whom Blake's life is unknown, it
may be well here to add a brief note respecting "the transitory
being that beheld this Vision."

Blake was born in 1757 and died before completing his
seventieth year, in 1827.[1] The world-wide importance of the
events of his day and the great work of his literary contemporaries
left him strangely apart. Though vitally interested in both, his
genius was of a kind to be almost as little moulded by them,[2] and

---

[1] The facts of Blake's life here told are to be found in the standard authorities such
as Tatham and Gilchrist. The complete list of references will be found in the Index
under "Blake's Life."

[2] It is true that events in America and France must be associated with a profound
change in Blake's mind that perhaps came to a head about 1800; just as he was con-
templating his removal to the country. But a revulsion of feeling, similar in origin to
Wordsworth's own, produced an almost opposite effect. While Wordsworth sternly
resolved to "inspect the basis of the social pile," Blake fled still further into his own
mind, convinced that salvation could only come from "within." *Cp.* Letter to Dr.
Trusler, 23rd Aug. 1799, "I feel that a man may be happy in this world," etc.
(Russell, p. 62) with his poem to Flaxman, 12th Sept. 1800, "Seeing such visions
[in America and France] I could not subsist on the Earth," etc. (Russell, p. 72).

quite as little of an influence upon them, as if he had lived in the Middle Ages.[1]

The son of an only moderately prosperous hosier, home-educated and with none but such opportunities as he discovered for himself of access to the limited culture of the London of his day, Blake even in his boyhood chose his masters from the ages. Isaiah, Milton, Raphael, Michael Angelo and later Shakespeare[2] were among the men who delighted and nourished his mind in the bud. Yet even in his teens he showed a poetic genius already too original to be merged in the character of these masters. At fourteen he was already "Blake"[3]—nay at four we hear of his first "vision," and throughout his boyhood of his seeing now a Hebrew prophet beneath a tree, now angels in the branches or among the haymakers in the early summer morning. On his death-bed he was still singing of heaven, still drawing and painting with undimmed powers of mind and hand.

But as his masters were picked from the centuries, so his admirers have hitherto been few and picked. Always unknown by the many, and largely ignored even by the literary, such men as Wordsworth, Southey, Coleridge[4] and Lamb[5] discovered him in

His scorn of "politics" is frequently expressed in his conversations with Crabb Robinson (Symons, pp. 255, 258, 262, etc.), cp. also note 2, p. 24 supra.

[1] This last does not apply to his pictorial art, which was "d—d good to steal from," as Fuseli wittily said (Gilchrist, i. p. 52). It is, of course, also true that Blake was enormously influenced by Swedenborg and others, though not by the great literary lights of his day—and not so as to affect the extraordinarily persistent character of his genius, whatever its mental diet or formal clothing.

[2] Vide poem to Flaxman (Russell, p. 71); and also Tatham's Life (Russell, p. 4)

[3] Vide poem, "How sweet I roam'd," etc., and Malkin's note that it was written before he was fourteen (Symons, p. 323).

[4] H. C. R. Letter to Dorothy Wordsworth (Symons, p. 276).

[5] Cp. Sampson (p. 97), Note to "The Chimney Sweeper," "S. of I.," and Gilchrist, i. p. 74. Also "H. C. R. Rem." (Symons, pp. 283-4).

his life, while Ruskin, the Rossettis and Burne-Jones have borne testimony in our own day to his extraordinary powers ; though it was only with Swinburne that the serious attempt was begun to decipher and understand him.

His first disciple and perhaps his only quite unconditiona one, was his wife. It is probable that she could neither read nor write when he married her,[1] and that she never pretended to understand his mystic system, but she gave Blake an unfailing wealth of pure devotion, and what he perhaps needed even more, an anchorage on earth, while Blake in exchange gave her heaven. He taught her to draw, to print off his engraved works from the plates and afterwards colour them, and even to see visions of her own. She alone kept his house or tenement ; joined his thirty- and forty-mile walks into the country ; rose at midnight to steady him under the tempestuous workings of artistic afflatus ; believed in him when no one else believed in him ; prayed with him when the very visions deserted him, and by her womanly skill, her innate sense of honour, her unfaltering courage and common-sense, saved him from worldly disaster and not seldom, perhaps, from his own extreme theories of life.

His profession of engraver was never pursued with marked success, yet though sometimes in great penury and at no time in affluence, he is said never to have been in debt ; and no genius ever lived a life of more spotless purity and honour in a world whose nature and ways were ever foreign to his mind.

One of the strangest features of this strange man is the mysterious eclipse from which he seemed to suffer in his middle

[1] The evidence for this generally accepted statement is that she signed her name with a cross in the marriage register (Gilchrist, i. p. 38). But as Symons points out, three brides out of seven on the same page did likewise (p. 46), so that we may possibly attribute the fact partly to nervousness.

life. The early lyrical genius of his boyhood did not last beyond life's early summer. The "Songs of Innocence" were published when he was thirty-two, and before he was forty his "happy pipe" was dropped, scarcely ever to be resumed.

Of a corresponding failure of his powers of expression in pictorial art, he was himself painfully conscious. And yet, the less his success, the more resolute he became to follow still deeper the direction his guiding spirit seemed to move in ; ever hoping and believing that the dawn was at hand when the course of his genius would appear justified before the world.[1]

It cannot be said that that dawn ever came for him during his life. Even by the very few who appreciated him he was less than half understood.[2] But during his later years his long-obscured genius did actually emerge in greater strength than ever, and it were hard to find a more beautiful chapter amongst the annals of art than the evening of his life spent in engraving these Job designs

---

[1] On 23rd Oct. 1804, he writes to Hayley : "I am really drunk with intellectual vision whenever I take a pencil or graver into my hand, even as I used to be in my youth, and as I have not been for twenty dark, but very profitable, years. I thank God that I courageously pursued my course through darkness" (Russell, pp. 171-2). And earlier he says in a letter to Butts (10th Jan. 1802) : "He who keeps not right onwards is lost" (Russell, p. 100).

[2] Tatham, to whom he left nearly all his unpublished MSS., sold or even burnt them all (Ellis and Yeats, vol. i. p. 167 ; *cp.* Garnett, "Portfolio," Oct. 1895, p. 70, and footnote, pp. 71 and 72). Palmer sold his invaluable MS. book for 10s. to D. G. Rossetti (*vide* Sampson's Bibliographical Preface to the Rossetti MS., p. 138). Gilchrist gives an amusing account of Varley's attempts to see Blake's visions, sitting by his side and looking up where Blake looked (Gilchrist, 1. p. 300). Crabb Robinson says ("H. C. R. Diary," 10th Dec. 1825): "Among the unintelligible sentiments which he was continually expressing is his distinction between the natural and the spiritual world." And again (24th Dec.): "The same half crazy crotchets about the two worlds—the eternal repetition of which must in time become tiresome" (Symons, pp. 257 and 264). Probably Linnell understood him better than anyone, but he, too, was occasionally shocked by Blake's heresies (Gilchrist, i. pp. 370-1).

and in inventing the not less wonderful but unfinished and almost unknown illustrations to Dante's " Comedy."

The room in Fountain Court, Strand, in which he and his wife worked, cooked, ate and slept, was lighted by a large sash window in one corner. This overlooked a court, beyond which might be seen the Thames and the distant Downs of Surrey or Kent, and by his work-table before the window, was hung Albert Dürer's " Melencolia."

An old man now, tired and even listless in those rare moments when his hands must be idle; more liable month by month to attacks of prostration and pain, he sat or lay in his earthly home, and drew and sang and dreamed of heaven. He was still in poverty, but owing to Linnell's commission to engrave the present series of designs, he was spared the necessity to stave off hunger by engraving a set of Morland's pig and poultry subjects. Yet, despite poverty and neglect, the bitterness of disappointed genius was now almost entirely gone from him, and much of the virulence of his wrath against contemporary Philistinism was lost in his deep and tender pity for human failings. Gentle, strong and radiant, we may picture him in his last days telling this tale of human frailty, human courage and human love, primarily indeed for his own pure joy, but probably also with a mysterious faith that it was for the redemption of his fellow-men.

LETCHWORTH, *August* 1910.

INTRODUCTION

Blake and the Book of Job

The Book of Job had been loved and brooded over by Blake for many years before he completed the present series of Illustrations.[1] They are, therefore, permeated with many of his deepest thoughts and imaginations, and, probably, even without knowing it, he often wrests the story far from its evident intention, to make it conform with his characteristic conceptions of life. This has given, amongst other things, a deeply interesting unity to the whole, which contrasts markedly with the wealth of diverse and often contending thoughts, that have found their way into the Hebrew book as we now have it.[2]

But though the points in which Blake departs from his original, are radical enough, they do not make as fundamental a change in the conception of the story as would at first appear. And in our attempt to fathom Blake's new reading we must not forget that

---

[1] *Vide supra* Preface, p. 16, note 1.

[2] " It has been thought that the descriptions of Behemoth and Leviathan [Job] 40, v. 6-41, v. 34, are later additions to the book . . . the prologue, 1-2, and epilogue, 42, vv. 7-17, have likewise been regarded as the work of later hands ; they are in prose, while the rest of the book is in poetical form. . . . More serious doubts attach to [Job] 32-37. The speeches of Elihu . . . [Job] 27, vv. 11-23, are also quite unsuitable to the argument of Job, they prove what he has been denying and the friends asserting, that the wicked always suffer an evil fate . . . [Job] 28. This chapter forms by itself one of the most beautiful poems in the Old Testament, but it has no connection with its present context ; " and so forth. (These extracts are from Prof. Weatherall's manual, " The Books of the Old Testament," pp. 107 *ff.*).

beneath his wonderful creation—for the work is nothing less—lies the same elemental humanity as in the old Hebrew story ; for Blake too, Job's history is that of a good man, led through disaster and despair to a final triumph in the loss of self, and the apprehension of an immeasurable, mysterious good behind the visible creation.

To understand Blake's book, therefore, we must briefly survey the book of Job as Blake found it in the Authorised Version.[1] This, it will be remembered, begins with a narrative introduction and ends with a short conclusion of a similar character, and it is in these portions that nearly all the incidents of the story occur. But the long poetic dialogue that includes the greater part of the book is philosophical rather than narrative, and is, in fact, an exalted protest against shallow solutions of the problem of suffering. Job's friends are made to voice the popular idea that if he suffers, it follows he must have sinned. Job indignantly denies this, and is represented throughout as a man whose terrible misfortunes are in bewildering contrast to his real deserts. In the end, it is true, he is overwhelmed by the manifestation of Jehovah's power. But though in his humiliation he "abhors" himself and repents, it is not for any moral failure to obey God's *laws*, only for a certain intellectual presumption in expecting to understand His *ways*. The Deity Himself makes no charge of sin against Job, and only convicts him of folly in aspiring to understand.

This ending leaves the problem of suffering as a sublime but unsolved mystery. And to the system-maker as such, every unsolved mystery is a menace to his system. Blake was an avowed system-maker. "I must Create a System," he says, " or be enslav'd by another Mans."[2] And therefore we must expect to

---

[1] *Vide* Appendix G for Summary of the Book of Job.   [2] "J^m.", p. 10, l. 20.

find him resolutely attempting to solve the problem that has been purposely left as a mystery by the Hebrew poet.

But even in the poem itself, as we now have it, there has crept in an episode of later composition, evidencing this tendency of system-makers to allow no ragged edges of unsolved mysteries. After the silencing of the three friends, a fourth has accordingly been introduced, who attacks Job on a new line. "There can be no reasonable doubt," says Canon Driver, that "the speeches of Elihu" are "not part of the original poem of Job : they are the addition of a writer who desired to develop certain considerations which did not seem to him to have been sufficiently emphasised by the three friends."[1] Elihu declares that God's justice precludes the idea of Job's innocence, and points out that he has at all events clearly sinned in word, if not in deed. "For he addeth rebellion unto his sin . . . and multiplieth his words against God."[2]

Now Blake with far greater sympathy, but doubtless from a similar motive, undertakes to show us Job's error, and instinctively selects Elihu's speech as the turning-point in Job's conversion and subsequent regeneration.[3] To him too, suffering was consequent upon error,[4] and his system obliged him to see Job as a profoundly mistaken man from the first. He therefore misses what is in a sense the dominant thought and purpose of the poem. But his treatment is so great on its own lines, and so original, that one cannot regret his failure to interpret correctly a work that had no need of Blake's art, to add to its enduring greatness.

In classing Blake with the accusing friends, however, it must

[1] "The Book of Job in the Revised Version," edited by S. R. Driver, D.D., etc. (Oxford), p. 93.
[2] Job, 34, v. 37.
[3] *Vide* Illus. 12, where all the marginal texts are from Elihu's speech.
[4] *Vide*, for instance, the passage in "J^m.", p. 36, ll. 43-55, especially ll. 49-53.

be understood that he did not accuse Job as they did, of wrong
actions, but rather of wrong ideas. A man's thoughts were
regarded by Blake as the real acts,[1] and mistake or *error* was to him
the only evil.[2] Indeed Job is, for Blake no less than for the
Hebrew writer, a truly great and good man fallen under the power
of Satan. But the fiend is a false and misleading creed in Job's
own mind and life, personified only for symbolic purposes. This
false creed undoes him at every turn, wrecking his happiness and
making his very goodness spiritually barren. "Devils are False
Religions,"[3] Blake says, and we shall find that Satan in the Job
Illustrations represents primarily a false reliance upon external
things. To Blake the only source of true good is the indwelling
divine spirit of man, which in some of his early work he calls the
Poetic Genius,[4] but later the Divine Humanity,[5] or according to
his context simply "God," or "Christ," or the "true"[6] or
"Eternal" Man,[7] all being essentially within.[8]

Job's misfortunes then appeared to Blake to be the true consequences of a mistaken faith in external acts or possessions. He
is undone, not by his vices, but by the very things which in the
Old Testament are told as his chief glories ; his material wealth,
his frequent burnt-offerings for sin, his ceremonial solicitude for
his immediate family, even his material gifts to the poor.

I shall hope to show in the following pages that this theme is

---

[1] "Thought *is* act," "Bacon," *vide* Gilchrist, i. p. 316; also "V. L. J.":
"Mental things are alone real" (Gilchrist, ii p. 200), etc., etc.
[2] "H. C. R. Diary," 17th Dec. 1825 (Symons, p. 262).
[3] "Jm.", p. 77.
[4] "N. N. R. (b) "; Notes to Swedenborg's "Angelic Wisdom." "M. H. H."
[5] The two are identified in "Mn.", p. 12, ll. 1-2.
[6] "N. N. R. (b)".
[7] "Jm.", p. 55, l. 9, etc., etc.
[8] "Jm.", p. 4, ll. 1-20, etc., etc., *vide supra* note 2, p. 24.

consistently worked out by Blake in his Illustrations. The
destruction of Job's sons and daughters, which is the climax of
Satan's first attack, is I think clearly represented as the blighting
of all domestic happiness and love when these are founded upon
success in the struggle for material prosperity, or to use Blake's
own expressive phrase, the attempt "to freeze Love & Innocence
into the gold & silver of the Merchant."[1] Again I shall show
reasons why Satan's later attack upon the person of Job himself
cannot be regarded as the infliction of physical disease, as in the
Bible, but of a subtle spiritual disease, essentially due to Job's
belief in the virtuousness of his practice of material beneficence, to
which he heroically clings even in his own extreme need. And
here Blake tenfold emphasises his point by making Job's outward
act so entirely noble. He shows Job, indeed, sharing his last
meal with a beggar.[2] Nothing could be more supremely right in
itself. But even this act can be tainted by a false idea of its merit.
To have spiritual worth, such an act must be one of pure humanity
and love with no more *virtue* in it, or even conscious sacrifice, than
a mother's sharing of her meal with her child. But Job is driven
by his sufferings to cite his pity for the poor as an instance of
righteousness such as ought, he thinks, to entitle him to the mercy
of heaven. "Did I not weep for him who was in trouble," he
pleads, "Was not my Soul afflicted for the Poor?"[3] But this
plea, on his own behalf, betrays his belief that merit may be gained
in the eyes of heaven by gifts of those material necessities of life
which are "Common to all in [Christ's] Kingdom."[4] Elsewhere
Blake has spoken in sufficiently scathing terms of the treatment of

---

1 "Jm.", p. 64, l. 23.   2 Illus 5.
3 Marginal text. Illus. 5.
4 Paraphrase of Thornton's "Lord's Prayer." (*Vide* E. & Y., 1. p. 126.)

the poor by the rich, and of the meagre doles of charity by which
he considered they bolstered up a state of society so greatly
advantageous to themselves.[1]   But here he shows that the same
false attitude of mind may exist even in extremest poverty, and
that in sharing our last meal, we may share it rightly or wrongly.
In his most nearly contemporary manuscript[2] Blake, describing how

[1] "Compell the poor to live upon a Crust of bread by soft mild arts,
    So shall we govefrin over all : let Moral duty tune your tongue ;
    But be your hearts harder than the nether millstone.
    Smile when they frown, frown when they smile ; and when a man looks pale
    With labour & abstinence say he looks healthy & happy.
    And, when his children sicken, let them die ; there are enough
    Born, even too many, & our Earth will be overrun
    Without these arts.   If you would make the poor live with temper,
    With pomp give every crust of bread you give, with gracious cunning
    Magnify small gifts : reduce the man to want a gift, & then give with pomp.
    Say he smiles if you hear him sigh.   If pale, say he is ruddy
    Preach temperance.   Say he is overgorg'd, & drowns his wit
    In strong drink , tho' you know that bread & water are all
    He can afford   Flatter his wife : pity his children ; till we can
    Reduce all to our will, as spaniels are taught with art."
(The "Four Zoas," as quoted by Sampson, pp. 350-351) cp. "Vala," vii.
ll. 117-129.

    "And Los prayed and said, O Divine Saviour arise
    Upon the Mountains of Albion as in ancient time, Behold !
    The Cities of Albion seek thy face, London groans in pain
    From Hill to Hill, & the Thames laments along the Valleys :
    The little Villages of Middlesex & Surrey hunger & thirst,
    The Twenty-eight Cities of Albion stretch their hands to thee :
    Because of the Opressors of Albion in every City & Village ;
    They mock at the Labourers limbs ! they mock at his starvd Children,
    They buy his Daughters that they may have power to sell his Sons .
    They compell the Poor to live upon a crust of bread by soft mild arts ,
    They reduce the Man to want : then give with pomp & ceremony.
    The praise of Jehovah is chaunted from lips of hunger & thirst."
                                        ("Jm.", p. 30, ll. 21-32.)
[2] "V. L. J.," vide supra note 1, Preface, pp. 19, 20.

devils "torment the just," says, "He who performs works of mercy, in any shape whatever, is punished and, if possible, destroyed—not through envy, or hatred, or malice, but through self-righteousness, that thinks it does God service, which god is Satan."[1] Satan in this case being what Blake calls the "Great Selfhood,"[2] that is, the outward and corporeal man, rather than the inner divine spirit, which is perfect love.[3]

Satan, as such, has now done his worst; but at this point the friends are introduced, and Blake's use of these in the development of his theme, while making no great departure from the Bible narrative, is nevertheless highly characteristic and original. True friendship is for Blake the home and refuge of man. "The bird a nest, the spider a web, man friendship,"[4] he says.

But Job's would-be comforters only serve to drive home to him the utter inhumanity of his own creed, by showing it him as it appears in others. For this "corporeal" faith which Job shares with his admonishers, makes enemies of would-be friends,[5] and the longer Job and his "miserable comforters" are together, the more they offend and exasperate one another, till at last Job, in desperation, appeals to God Himself, and discovers, in a terrible vision, that the God he has called upon is his own Satanic and "corporeal" self.

Such in outline is the story of Job's descent into the pit, as conceived by Blake. We must now try to explain equally briefly his conception of Job's re-ascent.

[1] Gilchrist, ii. p. 199.   [2] "Jm.", p. 33, ll. 17-18, etc.
[3] "For Man is Love, as God is Love" ("Jm", p. 96, ll. 26-27, etc., etc.).
[4] "M. H. H.," p. 8.
[5] "Corporeal friends are spiritual enemies" ("Jm.", p. 30, l. 10, and elsewhere; vide infra note 2, p. 76, Illus. 7).
[6] Vide Illus. 11.

As Satan primarily represents the external world and a man's materialistic ideas, so God represents true spiritual vision and the true inner reality of life. For the reality of anything is always the inner spiritual reality. The outward forms of things are mere illusions apart from their spiritual origins. In themselves they are no more than reflections in a glass.[1]

Now this inner reality is ultimately love, and the outward form of every man and creature is the expression of the indwelling spiritual love.[2] But we cannot love others in the abstract.[3] Love must be for definite individuals and their definite characteristics.[4] Therefore the very thing which makes us all one with one another,

---

[1] "The world of imagination is the world of eternity . . . the world of generation, or vegetation, is finite and temporal. There exist in that eternal world the permanent realities of every thing which we see reflected in this vegetable glass of nature." "V. L. J." (Gilchrist, ii. p. 187.)

[2] ("Jm.", p. 96, l. 26), etc.; and "The Divine Image," "S. of I."

Cp. "Seest thou the little winged fly, smaller than a grain of sand ?
It has a heart like thee : a brain open to heaven & hell,
Withinside wondrous & expansive · its gates are not clos'd,
I hope thine are not. hence it clothes itself in rich array :
Hence thou art cloth'd with human beauty, O thou mortal man.
Seek not thy heavenly father then beyond the skies : "
("Mn.", p. 18, ll. 27-32.)

[3] "He, who would do good to another, must do it in Minute Particulars
General Good is the plea of the scoundrel hypocrite & flatterer."
("Jm.", p. 55, ll. 60-61.)

[4] "He, who would see the Divinity must see him in his Children
One first, in friendship & love" ("Jm.", p. 91, ll. 18-19).

"The worship of God is, Honouring his gifts in other men each according to his genius, and loving the greatest men best, those who envy or calumniate great men hate God, for there is no other God" ("M. H. H.," pp. 22, 23)

Cp. "It is easy to acknowledge a man to be great & good while we
Derogate from him in the trifles & small articles of that goodness :
Those alone are his friends, who admire his minutest powers "
("Jm.", p. 43, ll. 56-8)

can only do so, by emphasising and particularising the individuality in each.[1] But in striving to perfect his *own* individuality Job had reduced it to a mere ephemeral appearance,[2] whereas, once he forgets himself in the pure passion for some fellow-creatures, his own individuality will be resurrected in him as the Divine-life itself.[3]

Accordingly, the crisis in Job's life is brought about by Elihu, who, according to Blake, rebukes Job, not for sin as the others did, but for the importance he has attached to his own struggles after an external and isolated perfection.[4] Even the outward world shows us the light of life shining in innumerable forms of men and

[1] " All broad & general principles belong to benevolence
Who protects minute particulars, every one in their own identity."
("J^m.", p. 43, ll. 22-3.)

And *vide* further, Illus. 17
[2] *Vide* especially Illus. 10
[3] *Vide* Illus. 18 and *seq.*

Cp. " So saying the Cloud overshadowing divided them asunder,
Albion stood in terror : not for himself but for his Friend
Divine, & Self was lost in the contemplation of faith
And wonder at the Divine Mercy & at Los's sublime honour.

Do I sleep amidst danger to Friends ! O my Cities & Counties
Do you sleep ! rouze up : rouze up. Eternal Death is abroad.

So Albion spoke & threw himself into the Furnaces of affliction.
All was a Vision, all a Dream . the Furnaces became
Fountains of Living Waters flowing from the Humanity Divine."
("J^m.", p. 96, ll 29-37.)

[4] An examination of the marginal texts to Illus. 12, shows that Blake does not emphasise Elihu's chief point, which is, that Job, in defending himself, is accusing God, and thereby finally putting himself in the wrong (Job 33, vv. 8-13). The only reproach which Blake records is from a supporting argument of Elihu's, to the effect that God, being removed from the possibility of suffering at Job's hands, cannot be motived by resentment or anything short of pure justice in His treatment of Job. Blake

things besides ourselves ; and the attempt to find life's purpose in
the saving of our single souls, is to be blind to the universal Spirit,
even as it is faintly manifest in the outward world.[1]

Thus aroused, Job once more sees a vision of his own eternal
individuality, but now his single personality is no longer the goal
of life for him, it is rather its key.   Nature, which before seemed
so cruel and oppressive, now becomes transparent to him, and he
sees the universe instinct with a life ultimately the same as his own.
God speaks to him out of the whirlwind in the likeness of himself,
but it is Job's transfigured self; for it has been found no longer as
dwelling in his single corporeal frame, but in all things.[2]

Into this greater, or rather deeper life, Job has now to learn to
enter, giving himself wholly to it and receiving all his joy, both
spiritual and corporeal, from it.   The right receiving is no less
necessary to the perfect humility of love than the right giving, for
to " live in perfect harmony in Eden the land of life," man must
both give and receive.[3]

From this point on, though still using the Bible story, Blake
becomes too intent on his own message to follow closely the
original.   His theme is now expanded in an almost unbroken

imagines this to be a condemnation of Job's", "principles of moral individuality "
(" M¤.", p. 7, l. 26).   "If thou sinnest, what doest thou against him, or if thou be
righteous, what givest thou unto him?"   Illus. 12; cp. Job 35, 6-7.

    Cp. " I care not whether a Man is Good or Evil; all that I care
        Is whether he is a Wise Man or a Fool.   Go! put off Holiness
        And put on Intellect " (" Jm.", p 91, ll. 54-56).

    Cp. " Striving to Create a Heaven in which all shall be pure & holy
        In their Own Self hoods " (" Jm.", p. 49, ll. 27-28).

[1] Vide Illus. 12.

[2] Vide Illus. 13, and the conceptions of " Essence " and " Identities," treated in
Illus. 17.

[3] " Jm.", p. 38, ll 21-22.

series of Divine visions.   We see Satan and the Satanic elements of
Job and his wife, finally cast out, before the judgment-seat of
Christ, the Divine-Humanity.[1]   The Christ then comes to earth,
and, as he blesses the patriarch and his wife, they behold in him
the beatific vision.

We next see Job's own earthly life, as symbolised by a sacri-
ficial flame, soaring up into the Divine life, which has become a
white sun of pure light.[2]   The two lives are now united in Job
himself, who is henceforth seen as the true image of God, in
virtue of his perfect loss of self, in love of his fellow-men and
of every creature in the divinely human universe.[3]

[1] " Forgiveness of sin is only at the judgment-seat of Jesus the Saviour, where the
accuser is cast out."   " V. L. J." (Gilchrist, ii. p. 199).

[2] Illus. 18.

[3] *Cp. supra* passage quoted in note 3, p. 41, describing Albion's self-surrender on
behalf of his friends, and then his consequent resurrection as the embodiment of God,
as described in the following lines .—

" So spake the Vision of Albion & in him so spake in my hearing
The Universal Father " (" Jm.", p. 97, ll.5-6, etc.).

NOTE ON THE MARGINAL TEXTS.

THE marginal texts were added after Blake had already made two complete coloured versions of the series. They are all quotations from the Bible, though frequently modified in some way. The less important of these modifications appear to be due to his having trusted his memory; but a few are intentional. They are of great value in helping to interpret the designs, but it must not be forgotten that ultimately *the texts are to be interpreted by the designs and not vice versa ;* for Blake regarded the literal meaning of Scripture as misleading, and the purpose of the illustrations is to give Scripture its spiritual interpretation.[1]

References for the texts are as follows :

I.	Illus	(1)	Mt. 6^{9} & Lk. 11^{2}
		(2)	Job 1^{5}
		(3)	Job $1^{1,2}$
		(4)	2 Cor 3^{6}
		(5)	1 Cor. 2^{14}
II.	,,	(1)	Dan 7^{9}
		(2)	Job 1^{8} or 2^{3}
		(3)	*cp.* Is. 63^{9}
		(4)	*cp.* Job 19^{26}
		(5)	Is. 64^{8}
		(6 & 7)	*cp.* Ps. 17^{15}
		(8)	Job 29^{5}
		(9)	,, 2^{1} (*cp.* 1^{6})
III	,,	(1)	,, 1^{16}
		(2)	,, 1^{12}
		(3)	,, $1^{18,19}$
IV.	,,	(1)	*cp* Job $1^{14,15}$
		(2)	Job 1^{7}, 2^{2}
		(3)	,, $1^{15,16,17,19}$
		(4)	*cp* Job 1^{16}
V.	,,	(1)	Job 30^{25}
		(2)	,, 2^{6}
		(3)	,, 2^{7}
		(4)	Gen. 6^{6}
		(5)	Ps. 104^{4}
VI.	,,	(1)	Job 1^{21}
		(2)	,, 2^{7}
VII.	,,	(1)	,, 2^{10}
		(2)	,, 2^{12}
		(3)	Jas. 5^{11}
VIII.	,,	(1)	Job 3^{7}
		(2)	,, 3^{3}
VIII.	Illus.	(3)	Job 2^{13}
IX.	,,	(1)	,, 4^{17-18} & 15^{15}
		(2)	,, 4^{15}
X.	,,	(1)	,, 23^{10}
		(2)	,, 19^{21}
		(3)	,, 13^{15}
		(4)	,, 12^{4}
		(5)	,, 14^{1-3}
XI.	,,	(1)	,, 30^{17}
		(2)	,, 30^{30}
		(3)	,, 20^{5}
		(4)	*cp.* 2 Cor. $11^{14,15}$
		(5)	*cp.* Job $7^{13,14}$
		(6)	*cp* ,, $19^{22,27}$
		(7)	2 Thes. 2^{4}
XII.	,,		all from Job 32-37
XIII.	,,	(1)	Job 38^{2}
		(2)	,, 38^{1}
		(3)	Ps. 104^{3}
		(4)	Job 38^{28}
XIV.	,,	(1)	,, 38^{31}
		(2)	Gen. 1
		(3)	Job 38^{7}
XV.	,,	(1)	,, 36^{29}
		(2)	,, 37^{11-12}
		(3)	*cp.* Job 40^{19}
		(4)	*cp.* ,, 41^{34}
		(5)	Job 40^{15}
XVI.	,,	(1)	,, 26^{6}
		(2)	,, 11^{7}
		(3)	Rev. 12^{10}
		(4)	Job 11^{8}
XVI.	Illus.	(5)	John 12^{31}
		(6)	Job 36^{17}
		(7)	Luke $10^{17,18}$
		(8)	1 Cor. 1^{27}
XVII.	,,	(1)	1 Sam. 2^{6}
		(2)	1 John 3^{2}
		(3)	Ps. $8^{3,4}$
		(4)	Job 42^{5}
		(5)	John 14^{9}, 10^{30}
		(6)	,, 14^{7}
		(7)	,, 14^{11}
		(8)	,, $14^{21,17}$
		(9)	,, 14^{20}, 14^{28}
		(10)	,, $14^{21,23,16,17}$
XVIII.	,,	(1)	Job 42^{9}
		(2)	,, 42^{8}
		(3)	,, 42^{10}
		(4)	Mt. $5^{44,45}$
		(5)	,, 5^{48}
XIX.	,,	(1)	1 Sam. 2^{7}
		(2)	Job 38^{41}
		(3)	,, 42^{11}
		(4)	Ps 136^{23}
XX.	,,	(1)	,, 139^{17}
		(2)	Job 42^{15}
		(3)	Ps. 139^{8}
XXI	,,	(1)	Rev. 15^{3}
		(2)	Job 42^{12}
		(3)	,, $42^{16,17}$
		(4)	Heb. 10^{6} and *cp.* Ps. 40^{6}

[1] *Vide* Preface.

ספר איוב

ILLUSTRATIONS of

The BOOK of JOB

Invented & Engraved
by William Blake
1825

London Published as the Act directs March 8 1825 by William Blake Nº 3 Fountain Court Strand

TITLE-PAGE

"Thus are the Heavens formd . . . in Eternal Circle, to awake the Prisoners of Death :
to bring Albion again . . . into light eternal, in his eternal day" ("Jm.", p. 75, ll. 23-26).

THE Hebrew words at the head of this page ספר איוב (Book of
Job) are possibly significant of the fact that these illustrations
do not represent the literal story so much as the spiritual meaning
of the Book of Job. For, according to Blake, the Hebrew Deity
was the Poetic Genius,[1] and to read the Scriptures in their literal,
rather than their poetic, sense, was to misread them.[2]

However this may be, there can be no doubt that the direction
of the angels' flight round the lower part of the design is symbolical
of Experience,[3] the process of the casting out of evil. For it will
be noticed that the angels on the reader's right are represented as
descending, those on his left as ascending, so that the whole train
moves clock-wise round the page. This is what Blake called " the
current of Creation,"[4] being the direction of the sun's apparent
motion as seen in the heavens.

We are in this book, however, concerned not so much with the
visible part of the current, which carries the sun in the daytime up

[1] " We of Israel taught that the Poetic Genius (as you now call it) was the first
principle and . . . that all Gods would at last be proved to originate in ours & to be
the tributaries of the Poetic Genius" ("M. H. H.," pp. 12, 13). *Cp.* also some
suggestions in note 4, p. 122, Illus. 18, respecting the significance of reversed writing
for Blake.
[2] " He understands by the Bible the Spiritual Sense. For as to the natural sense,
that Voltaire was commissioned by God to expose." " H. C. R. Diary," 18th Feb.
1826 (Symons, p. 267)
[3] *Vide* note 4, Preface, p. 21 and note 2, p. 127, Illus. 20.
[4] "Jm.", p. 77. *Vide* also Appendix C.

to his height in the south and down again into the west, but with the part below the horizon, by which the unseen sun is taken back through the under world, to re-appear again in the east.

This mysterious but triumphant passage through the night, speaks to Blake of the redeeming trend of human life, persisting even in our greatest darkness, and as such it was peculiarly descriptive of Job's fate.[1]

---

[1] Men are always moving. It is only the states they pass through that can be fixed   It is the work of Los in Jerusalem to fix states, in order to liberate individuals (*vide* note 4, Preface, p. 21).

"So Men pass on : but States remain permanent for ever " ("Jm.", p. 73, l. 43). *Cp.* "Jm.", p. 49, l. 70 *ff*; also "V. L. J." (Gilchrist, ii. p. 188).

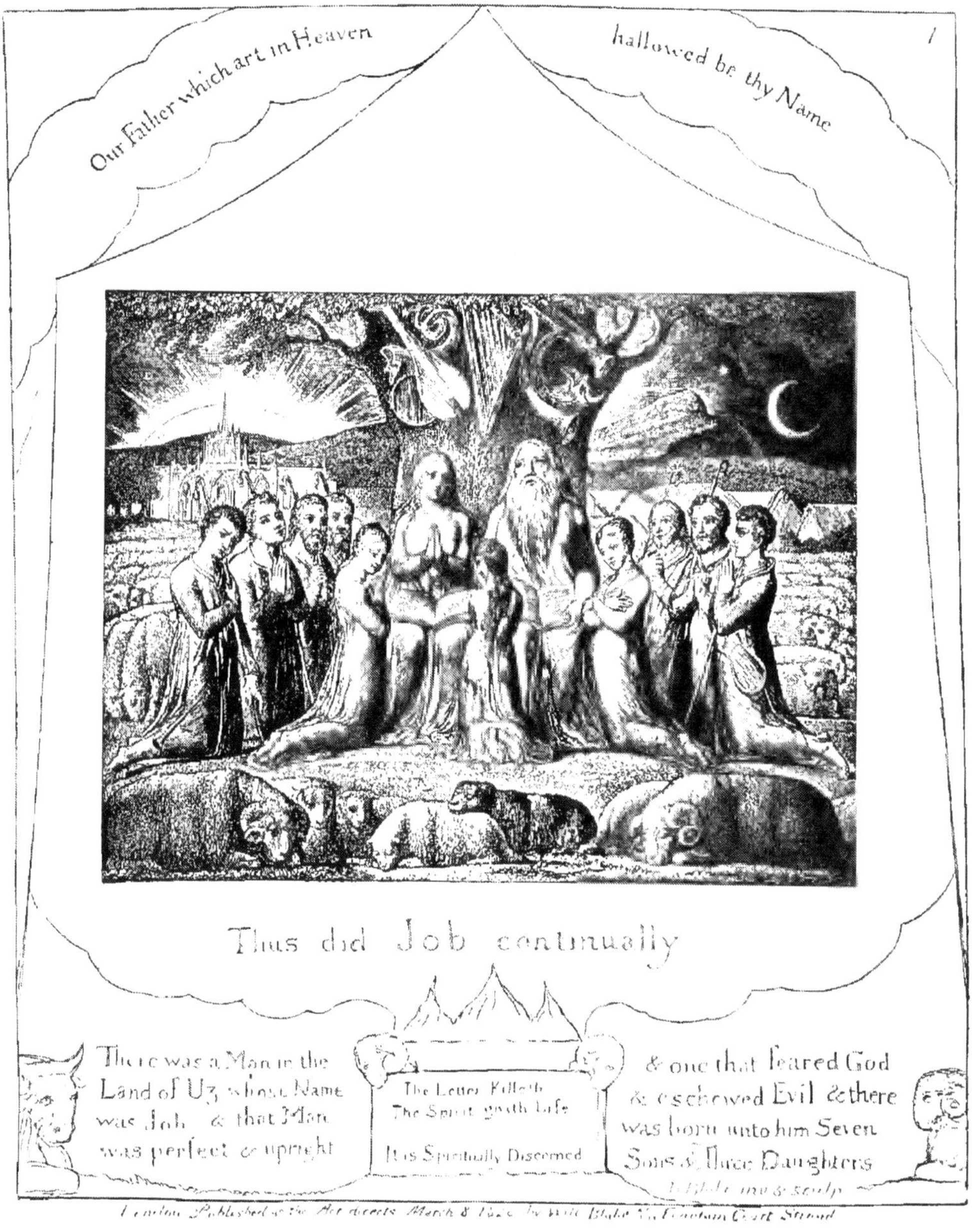
1
Our Father which art in Heaven
hallowed be thy Name
Thus did Job continually
There was a Man in the
Land of Uz whose Name
was Job & that Man
was perfect & upright
The Letter Killeth
The Spirit giveth Life
It is Spiritually Discerned
& one that feared God
& eschewed Evil & there
was born unto him Seven
Sons & Three Daughters

ILLUSTRATION I

" . . . the sweet regions of youth and virgin innocence ;
Where we live, forgetting error, not pondering on evil ;
Among my lambs & brooks of water, among my warbling birds :
Where we delight in innocence before the face of the Lamb ;
Going in and out before him in his love and sweet affection."
(*Cp.* also margin of next design, which also represents " Innocence ") (" Jm.", p. 20, ll. 6-10).

In the first Illustration we have the outward and visible life of Job portrayed. We see him gathered with his wife and children, for his evening devotions, the simple piety of which is suggested by the words in the margin above : " Our Father which art in' Heaven, hallowed be thy Name." Above them spreads a great tree, symbol possibly of Job's strongly rooted and prosperous mortal life ;[1] while in the background on his right, the pinnacles of a Gothic church rise into the arc of the setting sun.[2] On his

---

[1] In this book the tree is used where the design definitely refers to Job's experiences in the earthly plane.

Blake opens one of his early prophecies with " Eno, aged Mother," " sitting beneath the eternal Oak " (" Bk. of Los," ch. 1. vv. 1-2). " Vegetative " and " corporeal " are practically synonymous with Blake (" Jm.", p 77, etc. etc.). But I suspect that in these designs the " tree " has an ulterior meaning, and refers to his well-being, as expressed in material things. *Cp* " Good & Evil are Riches & Poverty a Tree of Misery." (" Laocoon," *vide* Illus. 2, 4 and 19; *cp.* " Jm.", p. 92, l. 25).

[2] If we had to attach importance to the phase of the moon this could only be a rising sun. But Blake's representations of Nature are always and deliberately ideal, *cp.* for instance the splendid display of the stars in Illustration 12, and its complete independence of astronomical considerations. *Cp.* " Natural objects always did and now do weaken, deaden and obliterate Imagination in me." " H C. R. Rem." (Symons, p. 300). Blake liked to begin with sunset and end with sunrise For those, however, who insist on realism, the fact that the scene represents sunset and not sunrise is sufficiently indicated by many of the animals being asleep and the men awake (*vide* Appendix C.).

left the crescent moon and evening star shed beneficent rays [1] upon his barns and storehouses. The two sides of the scene correspond to the spiritual (or "artistic") [2] and material sides of his life; both richly filled. In the foreground a few sheep are lying down with a dog, scarcely distinguishable from themselves, while numerous flocks are settling to rest or still gently grazing behind. A deep peace lies upon everything. The quaint musical instruments hang now silent upon the tree, and the dark shadows of the distant hills—presently to become so threatening—are as yet softened by the moonlight. The whole design represents the ideal state of Innocence, which the pastoral life symbolises. [3]

But Innocence is not a stable condition of the soul. And Job's "perfection" contains an element of death. The written books and the silent instruments above may perhaps be taken as corresponding respectively to the letter and the spirit, referred to on the altar below, and here we see Job dwelling on the letter that "killeth," while the Spirit that "giveth life" is not yet waked. [4]

The lines of the composition are very simple and strong, the backs of the recumbent sheep in the foreground forming a kind of soft but massive pedestal from which the figures rise in symmetrical undulations that meet and spread again in the great tree.

[1] *Cp.* last line of "Evening Star": "Poetical Sketches," London, 1783, p. 5.
   "The fleeces of our flocks are cover'd with
       Thy sacred dew   protect them with thine influence."
[2] "A Gothic church is representative of true art." "V. L. J." (*cp.* Gilchrist, ii. p. 192). "Christianity is Art," etc. ("Laocoon").
[3] "Jm.", p. 20, ll. 6-10, quoted *supra*, p 49.
[4] *Vide* last illustration, where the instruments are taken down and used.

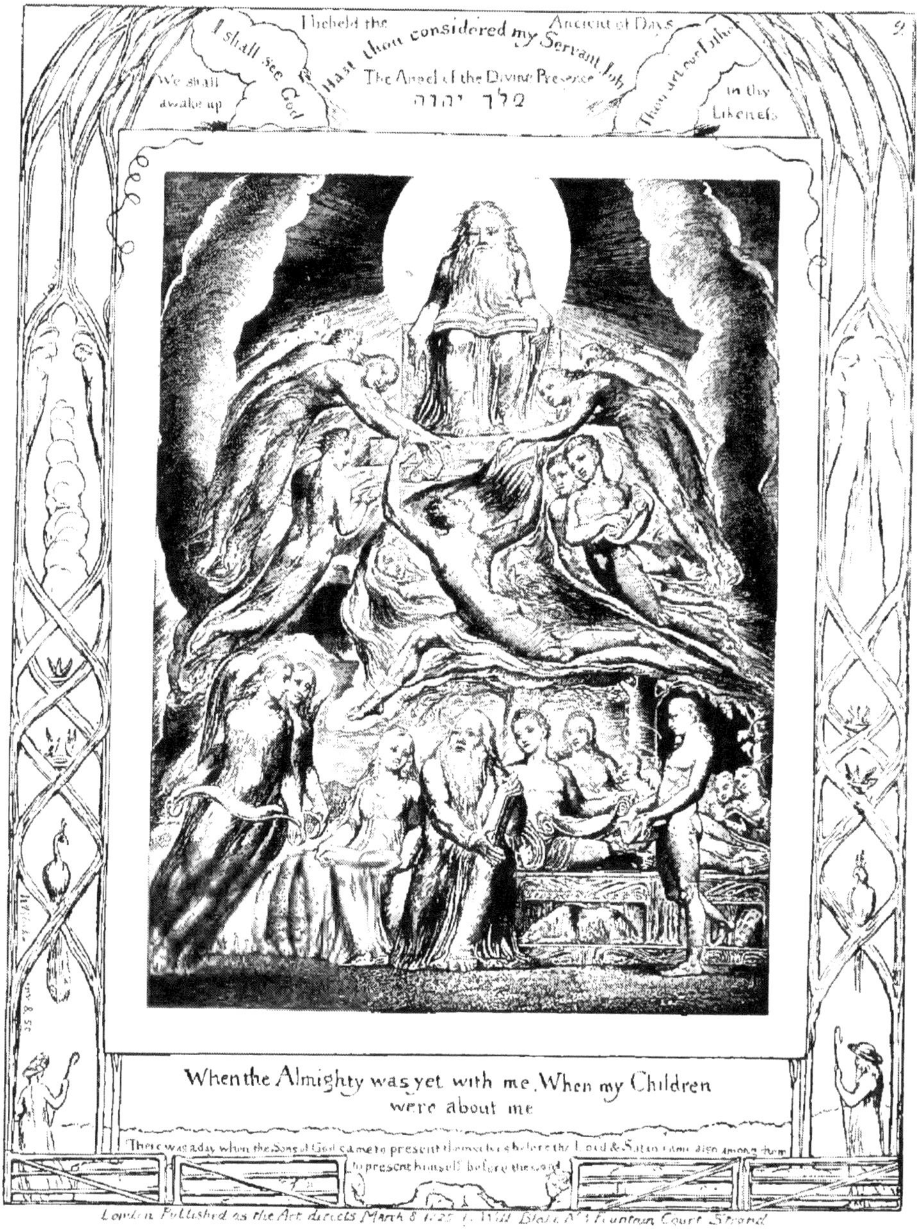
I beheld the Ancient of Days
I shall see God
Hast thou considered my Servant Job
The Angel of the Divine Presence
מלך יהוה
We shall awake up
Thou art our Father
in thy Likeness
When the Almighty was yet with me, When my Children were about me
There was a day when the Sons of God came to present themselves before the Lord & Satan came also among them to present himself before the Lord
London Published as the Act directs March 8 1825 by Will Blake No 3 Fountain Court Strand

ILLUSTRATION II

" Men are born with an Angel and a Devil." " Every man has a Devil in himself and the conflict
between his *Self* and God is perpetually carrying on." ("H. C R. Rem.," 1826.)

HERE the heavens are opened and we see into the spiritual life of
Job. For Blake represents the inner by the higher, "What is
Above," he says, "is Within."[1]

This inward life of Job is the real theme of the book, which
aims at explaining Job's outward story by revealing what according to Blake's vision was going on within. Accordingly Jehovah
and Satan must be conceived as representing aspects of Job's own
soul contending for victory. They are shown with their right
feet advanced to symbolise their spiritual correspondence with the
earthly man, who shows his left.[2] Here Jehovah is supreme
(מלך יהוה, Jehovah is King). He represents what Blake calls the
" Angel " or " Genius " (or more frequently the Poetic Genius) of
the man ; and for this reason he appears in the same image as Job
himself ; the two being intentionally drawn alike, because " The
Poetic Genius is the true Man . . . the body, or outward form of
Man is derived from the Poetic Genius," and " as all men are
alike in outward form, So (and with the same infinite variety) all
are alike in the Poetic Genius."[3] But though each man's genius is
his soul or self, it is at the same time something more. In it we
are enabled to approach the souls of all other men and things, and
" as all similars have one source,"[4] each man may ultimately reach
the origin (Father), the single essence of all things, through his
own " poetic genius."

[1] "Jᵐ.", p. 71, l. 6. [2] *Vide* Appendix A. [3] "N.N.R. (b)." [4] *Ibid.*

51

In other words, Blake, while conceiving that God is to each man his inmost being, yet believes that for a man to know his own being deeply enough is to be in union with the self of every other man and beast, and even flower and star throughout creation.[1]

God therefore is—as the marginal texts describe—both "Angel of the Divine Presence" and "Ancient of Days." For the ever-present consciousness of man is the same Divine force which, in other forms, has been working from the dawn of things in the worm and even the clod.[2]

The angels are reading the life-books[3] of Job and his family and carrying up the records to judgment. The Accuser,[4] too, rushes forward to bring his charge, and in his flame of selfishness we see the shadowy images of Job and his wife, suggesting that Job's spiritual life itself is a form of self-seeking.

[1] . . "Each grain of sand,
Every Stone on the Land,
Each rock & each hill,
Each fountain & rill,
Each herb & each tree,
Mountain, hill, earth, and sea,
Cloud, Meteor, and Star,
Are Men seen Afar."

Poem in Letter to Thos. Butts, 2nd Oct. 1800 (Russell, pp. 82, 83).

[2] "God is in the lowest effects as well as in the highest causes for he is become a worm that he may nourish the weak." "Lav.," 630 (Ellis, 620, p. 149).

"For everything that lives is holy, for the source of life
Descends to be a weeping babe;
For the earthworm renews the moisture of the sandy plain."

"F. Z." (*cp.* "Vala," ii. ll. 366-368).

Also *cp.* "Thel.," v. 3 with vv. 14 and 15 of poem on p. 27 of "Jm."

[3] *Cp.* "But still his books he bore in his strong hands, & his iron pen,
. . . . nor can the man who goes
The journey obstinate refuse to write"

"F. Z." (*cp.* "Vala," vi. ll. 164-172).

[4] Even in Blake's system Satan is the Accuser and Slanderer because "he torments the just, and makes them do what he condemns as sin, and what he knows is opposite to their own identity." "V. L. J." (Gilchrist, ii. p. 199).

ILLUSTRATION II 53

The convention by which in the first Illustration Job's spiritual good was shown on his right hand and his material good on his left, is maintained throughout the book wherever Job is drawn in the centre. And here his children in the flesh appear on his left, under "the Stems of Vegetation"[1] (always symbolical of earth), while the angels (probably intentionally including his wife, as we shall see[2]), are on his right.

Following the Bible story, Blake represents Satan's first attack as directed not against the man himself, but against his possessions and especially his family. In the next design we shall see how Blake seized the opportunity this offered for bringing home his indictment of selfishness against the family as an institution. In certain aspects it appeared to Blake to be a mere seeking immunity from the surrounding distress, which, so far from attempting to relieve, he believed it actually emphasised.[3]

With regard to the design as a whole, it suffers like so much of Blake's work from his theories. But as it is these also which give him his extraordinary originality and force, it seems ingratitude to complain. In this instance Blake's theory that in the true spiritual "Vision" everything appears detailed and definite,[4] has resulted in an over-elaboration, and massiveness, of the heavenly group. This is in some degree relieved by the rhythmic motion of the angels, and the disturbance caused by Satan's tempestuous inrush. This invasion by the Fiend comes like a first gust heralding the storm about to burst, and to shatter both the gentle domestic peace of Job's life shown below, and the passionless calm of his indwelling Deity, shown above.

---

1 " J^m.", p 60, l. 11, etc.
2 *Vide* Illus. 21, p. 132 and Appendix F   3 *Vide* Illus. 3.
4 *E.g* , " Vision is Determinate & Perfect." " Rey." 2 (Ellis, p 380), etc.

The margin is full of symbolism, the most important part of which is the representation of Job and his wife, as still dwelling in the pastoral age, or age of innocence.[1]

[1] "Jm.", p. 20, ll. 6-10; cp. note 3, p. 50, Illus. 1.   The significance of the Pillars of Fire and Cloud is more remote.   It is probably connected with the mythological characters of Luvah and his feminine counterpart Vala, cp. " Tho Valas cloud hide thee & Luvah's fires follow thee ("Jm.", p. 62, l. 28).   Luvah in separation, is perhaps love without "faith" or "intellect," and Vala "Mother Nature" without inspiration (Jerusalem), ("Jm.", p. 34, l. 9; "F. Z.," cp. "Vala," ii. ll. 104-105).

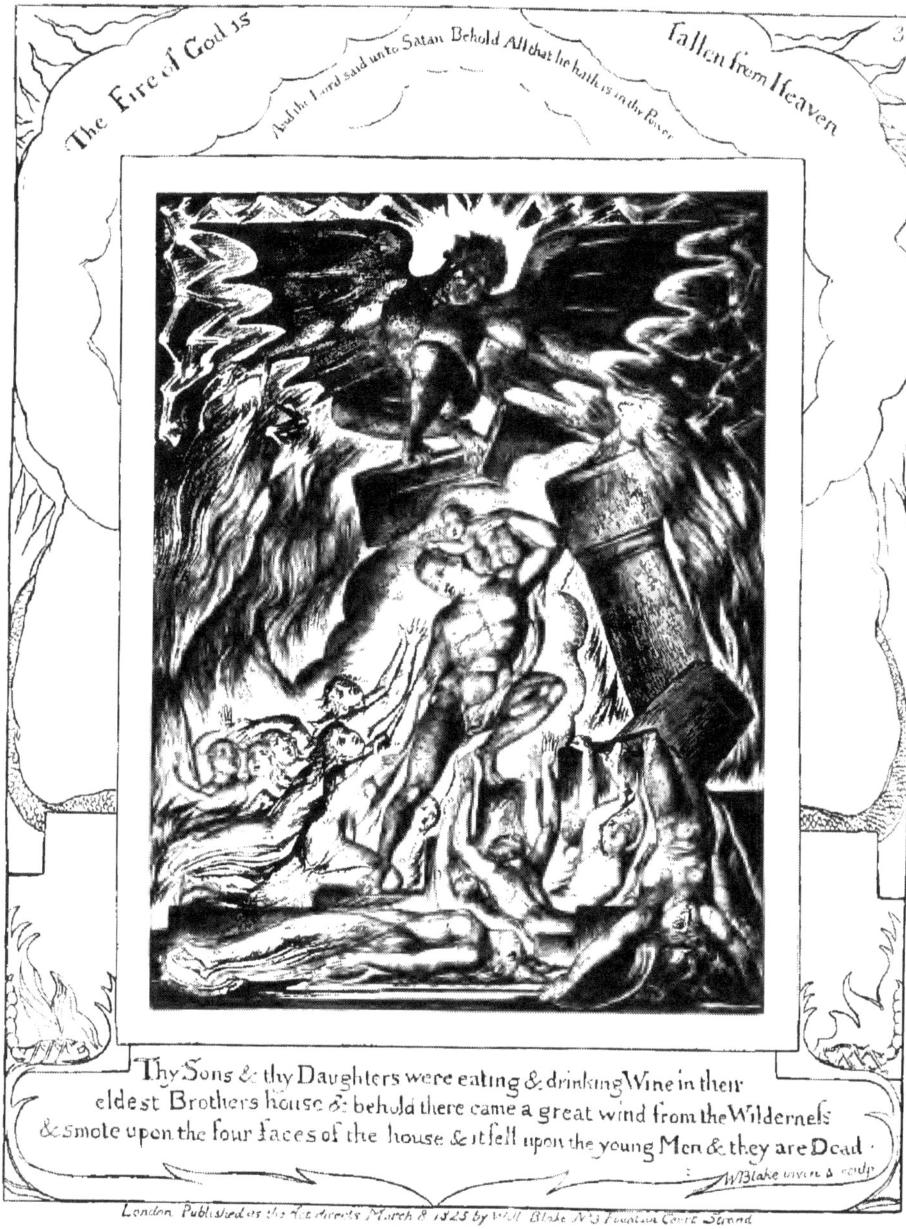

3
The Fire of God is fallen from Heaven
And the Lord said unto Satan Behold All that he hath is in thy Power
Thy Sons & thy Daughters were eating & drinking Wine in their eldest Brothers house & behold there came a great wind from the Wilderness & smote upon the four faces of the house & it fell upon the young Men & they are Dead
W Blake inven & sculp
London Published as the Act directs March 8 1825 by Will Blake No 3 Fountain Court Strand

ILLUSTRATION III

"The Devil is in us, as far as we are Nature." ("H. C. R. Diary," 24th Dec. 1825)

"Is this thy soft Family-Love
Thy cruel Patriarchal pride
Planting thy Family alone
Destroying all the World beside.

A man's worst enemies are those
Of his own house & family:
And he who makes his law a curse
By his own law shall surely die" ("Jm.", p. 27).

HERE Satan is shown working his will upon Job's children. "All that he hath is in thy power," says Jehovah. And the true source of that power lies, as we shall see, in the character of the patriarchal family itself. This is emphasised by a definite departure from the Bible narrative. There the three sisters are expressly mentioned as joining their brothers, whereas no word is said of wives or children. Here the seven sons are represented (all on one side of the design) with seven women obviously intended for their wives (on the other side; the side, namely, where Job's wife is generally placed); and the central figure holds a child.

The meaning, like the scene itself, centres round the main figure, who though furthest of all the men, from the foreground is drawn on a larger scale than any. Moreover, it is significant in a Blake design that he is the only man who shows his feet. This is connected with the extraordinary attitude of Satan shown above, who, as in the previous design, is truly within. The position of his legs not only enhances his demoniacal appearance and significance, but shows him to be definitely the spiritual prototype of the man he is crushing; as Jehovah, being dominant in the previous design, was the prototype of Job. For though Satan is shown with his left leg before his right, his right foot

in defiance of anatomical possibility, is drawn in advance of his
left, to make him in spiritual correspondence with the earthly
man, whom we see attempting to rise with left foot foremost.[1]

This symbolical attitude of the earthly man concisely expresses
Blake's fundamental charge against what he calls "thy soft Family-
Love, thy cruel Patriarchal pride."[2] The outwardly happy family, he
believes, is often spiritually vitiated by the attempt to escape evil and
attain happiness through material success ; and this, though it may
seem to rescue the few here and there, cannot touch the ultimate
source of distress.   It is what Blake would call the attempt to over-
come Babylon with the "natural" and not the "spiritual sword."[3]

Before further enlarging upon and substantiating this interpreta-

[1] Although out of piety to Blake we must "attend to the hands and feet" (*vide
supra*, Preface, p. 20), readers who find such technicalities confusing may, if they wish,
neglect them on a first reading. The argument will generally be sufficiently clear
without them, and even sometimes, perhaps, more convincing   In the end, it is to be
hoped, they will find, that the detailed symbolism has become genuinely expressive to
them, as it certainly was to Blake.

[2] "J^m.", p. 27, v. 20 of the poem.

[3] *Cp.* "J^m.", p. 52. "Babylon" is for Blake the "natural" as opposed to
Jerusalem the "spiritual" state of humanity. *Cp.* "Art thou not Babylon ? Art thou
Nature Mother of all ?" ("J^m.", p. 34, ll. 8-9). *Cp.* also "J^m.", p. 18, ll. 29, 30.
This state is described in the following passage :

"To build Babylon because they have forsaken Jerusalem
The Walls of Babylon are Souls of Men : her Gates the Groans
Of Nations : her Towers are the Miseries of once happy Families.
Her Streets are paved with Destruction, her Houses built with Death.
Her Palaces with Hell & the Grave ; her Synagogues with Torments
Of ever-hardening Despair squard & polishd with cruel skill.
Yet thou wast lovely as the summer cloud upon my hills
When Jerusalem was thy hearts desire in times of youth & love.
Thy Sons came to Jerusalem with gifts, she sent them away
With blessings on their hands & on their feet, blessings of gold
And pearl & diamond : thy Daughters sang in her Courts :
They came up to Jerusalem ; they walked before Albion."

("J^m.," p. 24, ll 30*ff.*)

ILLUSTRATION III   57

tion of the design, it may be well to recall Blake's unique method
of castigating evil, as shown for instance in some of the "Songs of
Innocence and of Experience." First he shows us a picture of the
thing as we see it with the outward eye (and as it truly is in
one aspect). This he does with all his matchless power of expressing fair and gentle thoughts. But against this delicate
background he then flashes his indignant picture of the same
thing as it ought to appear to us. The typical example of this
is his companion songs of Innocence and of Experience, entitled
"Holy Thursday." The first, it will be remembered, is a
beautiful lyric, describing the orphan procession entering St.
Paul's, and filling its dome with song. It breathes of gentle
and peaceful piety lifted to a genuine splendour :

> "The hum of multitudes was there, but multitudes of lambs,
> Thousands of little boys & girls raising their innocent hands.
> Now like a mighty wind they raise to heaven the voice of song
> Or like harmonious thunderings the seats of heaven among.
> Beneath them sit the aged men, wise guardians of the poor ;
> Then cherish pity, lest you drive an angel from your door."

Yet in his " Song of Experience " he asks in swift, scathing words :—

> " Is this a holy thing to see
> In a rich and fruitful land,
> Babes reducd to misery,
> Fed with cold and usurous hand ?
>
> Is that trembling cry a song ?
> Can it be a song of joy ?
> And so many children poor ?
> It is a land of poverty."

And so here, after showing us in the previous Illustration a
smiling picture of family bliss beneath the trees on Job's left,
where one of his sons reclines with his wife and three children,
he now proceeds in this design to show us what this family bliss

means if based on material good.   Yet there is this great difference
between Blake in his fiery youth and in his age.   In the present
design there is a depth of tragedy and horror expressed without
a trace of indignation.   The central figure, for all that he is
wholly possessed of Satan, is shown as genuinely heroic, and the
little child (badly as he is drawn) is shown touchingly clutching
hold of his father's hair.   With this in our minds as a corrective,
we must once more return to the " Songs of Experience " to learn
that Blake's charge against the family was essentially the same as
his charge against both Church and State.

Owing to false ideas, all alike, he thought, were based upon
(or at least permitted) a state of affairs in our streets and villages [1]
radically incompatible with the good they professed to foster and
protect.   Thus he tells how :

> " In every cry of every Man,
>   In every Infants cry of fear.
> In every voice : in every ban
>   The mind-forg'd manacles I hear.
>
> How the Chimney-sweepers cry
>   Every blackning Church appalls
> (originally—*Blackens o'er the churches walls*).[2]
> And the hapless Soldiers sigh
>   Runs in blood down Palace walls.
>
> But most thro' midnight streets I hear
>   How the youthful Harlots curse
> Blasts the new born Infants tear
>   And blights with plagues the Marriage hearse." [3]

---

[1] *Cp.* " Jᵐ.", p. 30, ll. 21-32, quoted at length, *supra*, Introd., note 1, p. 38.

[2] Sampson, p. 131.   This version (abandoned evidently so as not to repeat the
word " walls ") shows Blake's meaning to have been that the " cry " is a stain upon
the Church, making it (the Church) an object of horror.

[3] " London," " S. of E."

ILLUSTRATION III   59

So here, but in very different mood, Blake—using Job's children as types—shows how against even the momentary success of one man in his attempt to preserve the sanctity and immunity of the home, must be counted the headlong fall of the two brothers who have preceded him ; dashed amidst the cups and plates which symbolise their grosser passions ; and the beautiful ruined form of his sister, shown with her left hand upon a lyre, and her feet upon a tambourine (note the unnaturally raised left foot), symbolising the beauty and gifts that have been exploited for merely corporeal pleasure, reckless of the soul they were meant to express.

At the root of all this evil Blake believes is a false estimate of material things, which produces a financially-based Society, and puts in the hands of the wealthy a dire instrument of coercion, in the threat of destitution. He believed that there was food enough in the world for all,[1] and that what really bound men together was the poetic imagination and the love of the beautiful.[2] His delightful remark that " For every Pleasure Money Is Useless " is only the negative side of his charge. [3] Our belief in its efficacy, he holds, cuts us off from all the highest life. "Where any view of Money exists," he says, " Art cannot be carried on." [3] It even becomes the instrument of cruellest oppression, " the lifes blood of Poor Families," [3] for by its means we set " a Price . . . upon what is Common to all in [Christ's] Kingdom." [4]   " The

[1] " For Where-e'er the sun does shine
And where-e'er the rain does fall :
Babe can never hunger there,
Nor poverty the mind appall."
("Holy Thursday," " S. of E.")

[2] " Art and science [i.e. of course " visionary " science, not material, with Blake] the foundation of society." " V. L. J." (Gilchrist, ii. p. 196).

[3] " The Laocoon."

[4] Thornton (E. & Y., vol. i. p. 126).

whole Business of Man Is the Arts," he triumphantly declares, "& All Things Common." [1] Surely no Hebrew prophet could present a more unquestioning vision of the ideal, and Blake's childlike faith has something of the same haunting and purifying power.

But, unfortunately, the "Selfish Virtues of the Natural Heart" [2] as he believed, and the "soft family love" of the (apparently) successful man in the struggle, wed him to "the Laws of that Babylon which . . . shall shortly be destroyed, with the Spiritual and not the Natural Sword." [2] This age is the time prophesied by the eternals in Jerusalem, "when a mans worst enemies shall be those of his own house and family." [3] Yet "Poverty is the fool's rod, which at last is turned on his own back." [4] That is to say no man can really escape from the seething distress in which he allows the rest of the world to welter. So long as the distress remains, it is a stain and horror if not an actual menace to himself. Job's son may for a moment rescue his own wife and child from the sinking abyss of flame, but so long as he fights with the natural sword, and not the spiritual, the distress itself remains an ever-greedy abyss behind, and others whose need is no less dire must cry for help in vain. This is emphasised in the design by the repetition of the wife's attitude in the woman just behind her.

Now this "corporeal" view of life is inflicted and inspired by man's indwelling Satan, and the design not only represents a world of distress all around Job's son, but the blighting of his own domestic joy and happiness by the very system with which he vainly attempts to secure them. We see with what glee Satan

[1] "The Laocoon."   [2] "Jm.", p. 52.
[3] "Jm.", p. 46, ll. 25, 26
[4] "V. L. J." (Gilchrist, ii. p. 195).

ILLUSTRATION III   61

crushes the man beneath the pillars of his own house, and the
scene closely illustrates and interprets the angry verses in
" Jerusalem " :—

> " Is this thy soft Family-Love
> Thy cruel Patriarchal pride.
> Planting thy Family alone,
> Destroying all the World beside.
>
> A mans worst enemies are those
> Of his own house & family ;
> And he who makes his law a curse,
> By his own law shall surely die." [1]

One point remains to be noticed. The four men sinking in
the flames are drawn on a smaller scale than the other brothers.
This may be partly due to exigencies of space, and partly to the
desire to emphasise the importance of the central figure. But it
has further the curious effect of enhancing the nightmare appearance of the brother fallen head-foremost. His whole body is really
drawn in the foreground, but his knees are made to reach the
stone step behind the four sinking brothers, which gives an
additional monstrosity to his already weird figure. His right
hand is (no doubt purposely) cut off by the margin, and his left
hand curiously flattened, and apparently *nailed* against the plate,
so as to suggest the head-downward crucifixion referred to in
Blake's "Vision of Last Judgment." "The modern Church,"
he says, "crucifies Christ with the head downwards." [2] The
meaning of this passage is somewhat obscure, but it seems likely
to be that the imaginative and artistic temperament (symbolised by

---

[1] Jm.", p. 27, vv. 20, 21 of poem.
[2] " V L. J." (Gilchrist, ii. p. 197).

Christ)[1] is driven by the false ideals of the "modern Church," to express itself in sensual pleasure, the "woeful tree," upon which it is inverted and cruelly slain.   In other words, our false ideals often wreak the direst wreck upon imaginative natures, which in "Eternity" are the most divine.[2]   A closely associated idea is perhaps represented by one of the men in the pit, who looks as though he had been flung off the steps by his brother.   He appears to be wearing a crown of thorns, and probably represents an idea always near Blake's mind ; the ever-penurious artist, persecuted by the worldly and successful.   "Jesus & his Apostles & Disciples were all Artists," he says in the "Laocoon" texts.[3]

Flames, smoke and scorpions—whose envenomed tails impend

---

[1] *Cp* "The mocker of art is the mocker of Jesus," Letter to Hayley, 11th Dec. 1805 (Russell, p. 189).

[2] *Cp.* "Babylon, the Rational Morality, deluding to death the little ones, in strong temptations of stolen beauty" ("Jm.", p. 74, ll. 32, 33).

It is true that here and elsewhere the "temptations" may be intellectual rather than carnal, but the mere fact that Blake continually uses images of carnal ruin to describe mental disaster proves that he had the natural instinctive horror of the former.   His test is that of humanity ; where vice appeared to him cruel or dehumanising, he thinks of it as something unspeakably grievous and even diabolical.   It would be as false to regard him as non-moral (not to speak of immoral) because of the highly unconventional character of much of his moralising, as it would be to regard him as being without the religious sentiment because his Christianity frequently quarrels with the "orthodoxy" of his day.

[3] The connection in Blake's mind between "Natural" morality and the crucifixion, is shown by the passage on p. 52 of "Jerusalem."   "Natural Morality, or Self-Righteousness, the Selfish Virtues of the Natural Heart.   This was the Religion of the Pharisees who murder'd Jesus."

Cp. with this "Some people, and not a few artists, have asserted that the painter of this picture [A Vision of the Last Judgment] would not have done so well if he had been properly encouraged.   Let those who think so, reflect on the state of nations under poverty and their incapability of art.   Though art is above either, the argument is better for affluence than poverty; and though he would not have been a greater artist, yet he would have produced greater works of art, in proportion to his means." "V. L. J." (Gilchrist, ii. p. 195).

ILLUSTRATION III 63

(like "the fool's rod") above their own backs—with a glimpse of the scales of the serpent (money)[1] fill the margin. There is nothing obscure in the texts except perhaps the meaning of the words, "The fire of God is fallen from Heaven." In the Bible this text applies not to the destruction of the sons and daughters, but to that of the flocks and their shepherds. But Blake possibly used it here to describe the state when the divine energy of man (the fire of God) falls from his mind (Heaven)[2] into the lower centres of his life.

[1] "Money which is the Great Satan" ("Laocoon").

[2] *Cp.* "Bends over thy immortal Head, in which Eternity dwells" ("J^m.", p. 86, l. 10)

    Cp. "From out the Portals of my Brain, where by your ministry
       The Eternal Great Humanity Divine, planted his Paradise."
                      ("M^n.", p. 3, ll. 7, 8.)

And there came a Messenger unto Job & said The Oxen were plowing & the Sabeans came down & they have slain the Young Men with the Sword

Going to & fro in the Earth

& walking up & down in it

4

And I only am escaped alone to tell thee.

While he was yet speaking
there came also another & said
The fire of God is fallen from heaven & hath burned up the flocks & the
Young Men & consumed them & I only am escaped alone to tell thee

WBlake invent & sculp

London Published as the Act directs March 8 1825 by Wm Blake N 3 Fountain Court Strand

ILLUSTRATION IV

"What is the price of Experience? Do men buy it for a song?
Or wisdom for a dance in the street? No it is bought with the price
Of all that a man hath,—his house, his wife, his children" ("F Z.").

IT is a relief to escape with the messengers into the open air, despite
the depth of tragedy that awaits us in the grief of Job and his wife,
sitting beneath their tree and receiving the tidings of disaster in
close succession.

The symbolism of this design is comparatively simple. The
thatched barns are gone, only a remnant is left of the flocks and
herds. But as yet the Gothic church, symbolising the spiritual
wealth of Job's life,[1] still stands ; for the two messengers,[2] being
shown with left feet foremost, must be supposed to announce
material disasters only.

In the next and following designs the church is replaced by
Stonehenge-like erections and massive square-set masonry. These
symbolise what Blake calls the "Druidical" religion of Law and
Duty, as opposed to the Spiritual religion of Art.[3]

---

[1] *Vide* note 2, p. 50, Illus. 1.

[2] Blake, like the Greek sculptors, worked for himself and the Gods alone.
There is a third messenger on the sky-line, just under the knee of the first, and in
a good original, by the aid of a glass, one can see that this third messenger is unmistak-
ably represented with right leg foremost. His tidings are those of spiritual Death—
the death of Job's family under the curse of Satan.

[3] The lapse from Spiritual Innocence to Druidic Law, and then the rebuilding of
Jerusalem by Christ, is set forth in the poem on p. 27 of "Jm.", where the
golden pillars of Jerusalem (v. 1) give place to the "Druid Pillars" of Satan

In the margin above, Satan, whose back is turned, goes forth upon the earth with left foot advanced, and a sword in his left hand.   The little figures at the corners are Job's dead children.

(v. 10).   Satan, however, is reclaimed in verse 19, and in the present work a corresponding idea will be found in Illus. 18.

Cp.   "O pitious Sleep O pitious Dream : O God O God, awake I have slain
      In Dreams of Chasti(ti)ty & Moral Law I have Murdered Albion : Ah !
      In Stone-henge & on London Stone & in the Oak Groves of Malden
      I have Slain him in my Sleep with the Knife of the Druid."
                    ("Jm.", p. 94, ll. 22-25 ; cp. Ibid., p. 92, ll. 24-27, etc.)

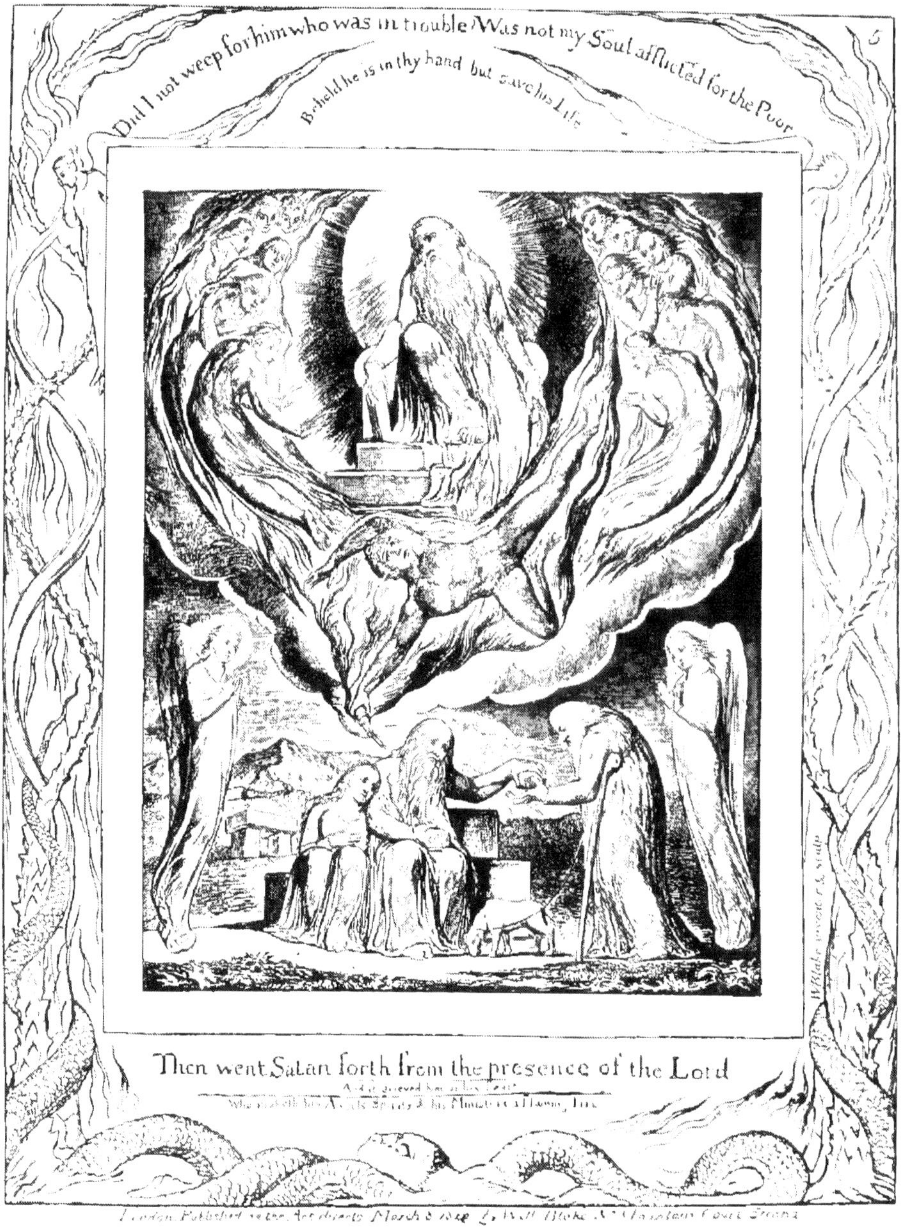
5
Did I not weep for him who was in trouble Was not my Soul afflicted for the Poor
Behold he is in thy hand but save his Life
Then went Satan forth from the presence of the Lord

ILLUSTRATION V

"Devils are False Religions" ("Jᵐ.", p. 77).
"Satan . . . drawing out his infernal scroll . . . upon the clouds of Jehovah, to pervert the Divine voice in its entrance to the earth . . Saying I am God alone, there is no other : let all obey my principles of moral individuality" ("Mⁿ.", p. 7, ll. 19-26).
"O Lord descend and save " ("Jᵐ", p. 45, l. 16)

IN order to understand this wonderful design, we must first turn our attention to Heaven, the seat of war in Job's soul. Here Satan has returned for fuller powers against the man he has set out to destroy, having failed to provoke him to impiety by the loss of all he possesses. In the Bible Satan's second onslaught consists in the infliction of "sore boils," which to our modern ears sounds like an anticlimax after the loss of sons and daughters. But Blake represents the second crisis as still more dire in its effects upon Job's inner world, than it is on the earth below. Satan almost succeeds in overturning Heaven and making it into hell. The contagion of his presence has infected the seraphs themselves, who are now seen bathed in flames like his own. He has gained some terrible power over Jehovah himself, whose whole figure betrays grief and suffering in strange contrast to his divine calm, as shown in the second Illustration, before his power had been deputed to the Fiend. There he sat remote and passionless, unmoved by the rush and rhythm of the rest of the design. Here we see him almost unseated and his halo half sunk beneath the shades of earth. Satan appears to have given a direful wrench to the stability of Heaven, carrying God downwards and leftwards, a motion resisted by the resolute thrust of the Deity's right foot and knee, and the planting of the book in his right hand, upon the steps of his throne.

67

The only place where the peace of heaven still lingers is upon earth, where Job calmly divides his last meal with a beggar, a deed at which the gentle angels gaze in love and wonder.

Blake's intention in introducing this episode, of which there is no suggestion in the Bible, is doubtless in the first place to show Job's unconditional victory over the first attack of Satan. Job rises heroically superior to the "cruel patriarchal pride," the false "family love," which undid his sons. The beggar is allowed to share equally with his own wife and himself, and even the dog must have its share of the crumbs. But Blake has a still subtler purpose in this episode. A lesser artist might have tried to establish his thesis of error in Job's life by representing him as guilty of some lapse from his ideal. This was the error of the friends, which Blake avoids, while at the same time he thereby increases the strength of his own indictment. He shows that the victim of false ideas may *do* right, but he cannot remove the taint of corruption in his *thoughts*, till he has removed the error itself; and our thoughts are our real acts.[1] Accordingly the one ominous sign upon earth is the replacement on Job's right of the Gothic church by a Stonehenge-like altar. This denotes what Blake calls "the Druid Temples of the Accuser of Sin,"[2] symbol of the "Druid Law . . . a False Holiness hid within the Center."[3] Job's error, therefore, is in doing from a sense of duty or "Law," what should be a free and unconstrained act of love. His own words quoted above in the margin are a subtle indication

---

[1] *Cp.* "Thought *is* act, Christ's acts were nothing to Cæsar's, if this is not so" ("Bacon," Gilchrist, 1. p. 316), etc.

[2] "J^m.", p. 98, l. 49.

[3] "J^m.", p. 69, ll. 39, 40, *i.e.*, of course, "The Selfish Center" ("J^m.", p. 71, l. 7). *Vide* also note 3, Illus. 4. *Cp.* "Stony Druids . . Sway'd by a Providence opposd to the Divine Lord Jesus" ("J^m.", p. 50, ll. 2 and 4).

ILLUSTRATION V 69

of this wrong mental attitude. "Did I not weep for him who was in trouble; Was not my Soul afflicted for the Poor?"—is, after all, a plea for himself, on the ground of his own righteousness and compassion. The insidious nature of Satan's assault is that he destroys Job not in his vices, but in his virtues, and the Fiend is symbolically depicted as drawing down the fires of the seraphs themselves to mingle with his own in the vial of torment and damnation.

In his "Vision of Last Judgment," describing how devils (whom he elsewhere declares to be "False Religions"[1]), "torment the just," Blake says: "He who performs works of mercy, in any shape whatever, is punished and, if possible, destroyed — not through envy, or hatred, or malice, but through self-righteousness, that thinks it does God service, which god is Satan."[2] The belief that in performing works of mercy in any form whatever, we are doing something meritorious, poisons every act of humanity, making it a subtly selfish attempt to save our own souls in the name of love and religion ; it is the worship after all of Satan in the belief that it is a tribute to God.

But it must further be noticed how this error of Job's is itself an effect of his materialism. It is Job's belief that we can have property in the material necessities of life, "in what is Common to all in [Christ's] Kingdom,"[3] that misleads him. The material nature of the gift is here doubly emphasised, for the episode is placed on the left side of the design (relative to Job and Jehovah), and the bread is both given and received with the left hand. To attribute virtue to *any* gift to a brother would argue a lack of spiritual perception. But there is a special sense in which the arrogation of

[1] "Jm.", p. 77.   [2] "V. L. J." (Gilchrist, ii. p. 199).
[3] Thornton (E. & Y., i. p. 126).

the right to bestow on our fellow-men the material necessities of
life is a usurpation by the Satanic selfhood of the bounty of
heaven.

> "For Where-e'er the sun does shine,
> And where-e'er the rain does fall;
> Babe can never hunger there,
> Nor poverty the mind appall." [1]

And this brings us to the critical point of the interpretation.
It is Job's misconception of the value and possibilities of material
things, and of the corporeal life, that makes him (all unwittingly)
erect his corporeal man into the place of Deity, as though it were
his to give or withhold a man's daily bread; and for the only time
in the book, the definitely earthly man is shown with the right
foot uncovered.   In all other places where Job's right foot is made
the more prominent, his spiritual man is not separately shown, and
both aspects are therefore included in the one figure.   Job is
attempting then to make a God and Heaven upon the earthly
plane.[2]   His effort is far nobler than his son's attempt to rescue
his individual family from the surrounding distress, but essentially
it is based on the same fallacy; a false conception of material
values.   The gentle angels that float on either side of Job, and
seem to give his act the seal of heavenly approbation, must not be
conceived of as individuals,[3] but are probably Job's own mild

---

[1] "Holy Thursday," "S. of E."

[2] *Cp.* "Striving to Create a Heaven in which all shall be pure & holy
In their Own Selfhoods" ("J^m.", p. 49, ll. 27, 28).

[3] Blake gives a reasoned justification for his love of personifying thoughts and
influences in his final note to Lavater's "Aphorisms" (Ellis, p. 151).   The argument
is concluded thus: "For these reasons [principally that—"It is impossible to think
without images of somewhat on earth"], I say that this Book is written by consultation
with Good Spirits, because it is Good."

ILLUSTRATION V   71

thoughts, by which he strives to guard and preserve his mundane heaven. "There is a constant falling off" of angels from God,[1] Blake says. And it is noteworthy how much less robust and virile these angels are than those around the throne, or indeed than any others in the book.

Before leaving this design, we must look once more at heaven. It is Job's Titanic attempt, the more dangerous for the very reason that it is so heroic, to make the things of earth usurp the place of heaven, that is the real secret of Satan's power above. Symbolically speaking, it is the appearance of Job's right foot on earth that necessitates the uncovering of God's left foot in heaven, in order that the balance of the Divine humanity, Satanically disturbed, may be restored. The Nemesis of all such efforts to create a righteousness of higher sanction than that of pure human love, is that "Attempting to be more than man, we become less."[2] Nevertheless, there is a kind of Providence in things—so Blake believed —which makes a man's actions produce the experience needed to purge away his errors.[3] And Job's bestowal "of all his goods to feed the poor," which is as yet wanting in perfect charity, is to lead him through the experienced pains of poverty to the "more excellent way." So far from his merit securing him against the material results of his act (as he pleads that it ought), it is those very results that are to bring home the needed lesson. In the sixteenth Illustration, where both God and Satan once more appear together with the earthly Job, the Fiend is finally hurled into the

---

[1] "H. C. R. Diary," 18th Feb. 1826 (Symons, p. 268).
[2] "F. Z." (cp. E. & Y., "Vala ," ix. 704).
[3] "for all things are so constructed
And builded by the Divine hand that the sinner shall always escape."
("Jm.", p. 31, ll. 30-31, etc.).
For further treatment of Blake's conception of the Divine ordering, vide Illus. 17.

abyss, and there have entered into the halo of Deity little figures of weeping angels that speak of true human compassion ; that touch of earth which becomes a feature of the Divine mind in virtue of the perennial act of incarnation, producing the inward knowledge of human suffering, so conspicuously absent in Job's Jehovah as he first appears (Illus. 2).

Job's wife is at this crisis a figure of ideal womanly fidelity. She loves her husband not for his possessions or position, or even for his alleged righteousness, but simply for himself. She sees from afar the consequences in this life of such acts as Job's, but while she looks wistfully at the bread they will soon so much need, she clings loyally to her husband's arm, ready to suffer everything with him.

In the margin the unveiled serpent now appears amidst thorns and flames.

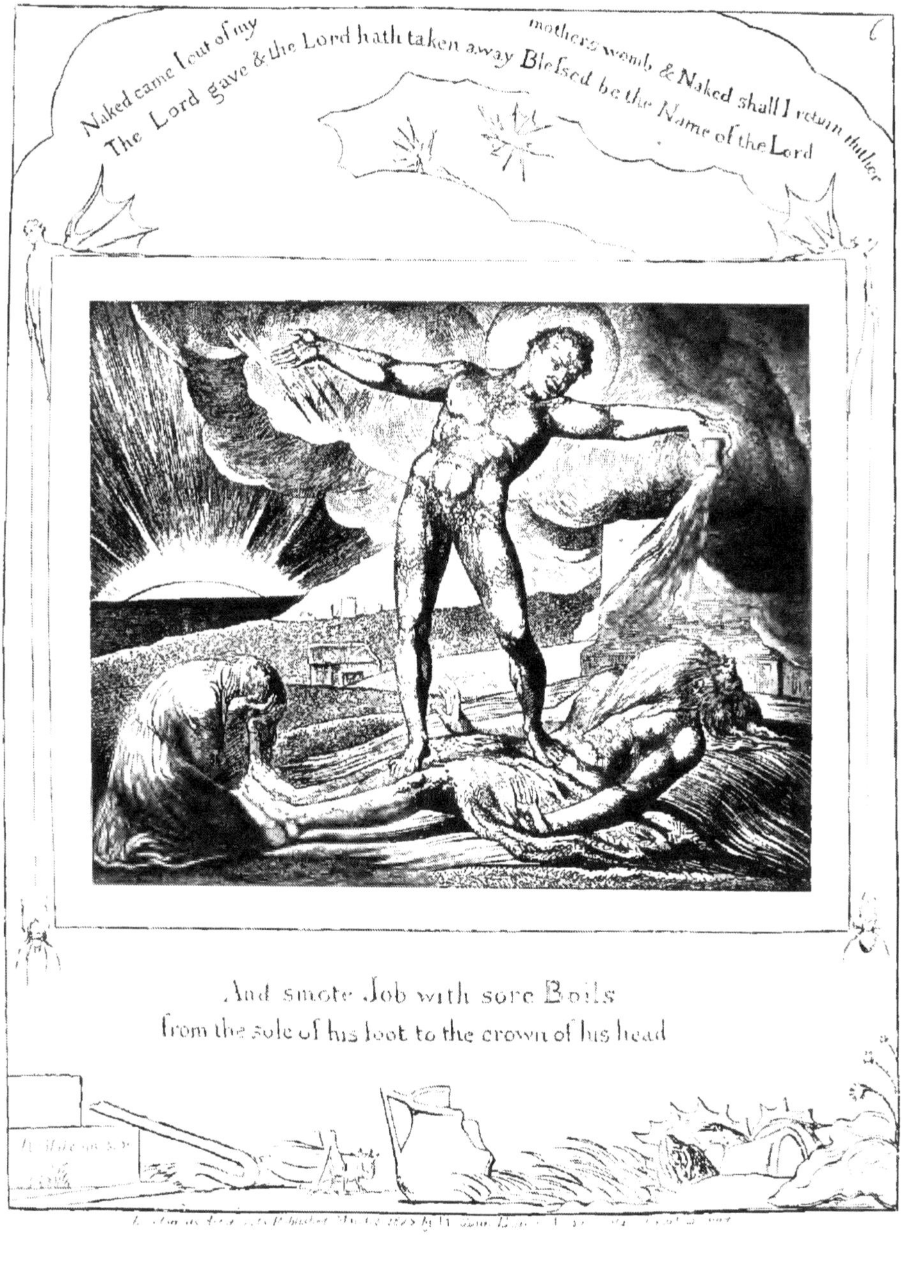
6
Naked came I out of my mothers womb & Naked shall I return thither
The Lord gave & the Lord hath taken away Blefsed be the Name of the Lord
And smote Job with sore Boils
from the sole of his foot to the crown of his head

ILLUSTRATION VI

"Every boil upon my body is a separate & deadly Sin" ("Jᵐ.", p. 21, l. 4).

THIS Illustration is one of the finest examples in Blake's work of his conventional use of landscape to express states of mind in his characters. The identification of the great cloud with Satan and his weapons combines the sense of immense and vague oppression with deliberate and concentrated venom. The whole heavens seem to descend on Satan's left, in ruthless and bitter hostility, while the light of day sinks in the black deluge on his right.

The detailed symbolism of the design is in this case less interesting than the design itself, but some of it has a certain importance in the development of Blake's conception of the story.

And first we must notice the extraordinary light on the knees of Job's wife. The light of life has fallen from Job's face to his feet, which illuminate his wife's knees, who, in her own despair,[1] still supports and cherishes the physical basis of his being. This probably symbolises the same fact as the Deity's dropped left foot in the preceding Illustration ; God has come down to the sorrows of

---

[1] It is a little surprising at first to see that Job's wife here shows her right foot. In all Blake's later designs it is very rare to find a woman showing her right foot *only*, and here it is probably indicative of some grievous dislocation of nature. Job's wife shows her left foot, even in regeneration (Illus. 21). The fact that it falls upon her to have to preserve the Divine Light from complete annihilation, is part of the confusion wrought by Satan. *Vide* Appendix A.

earth,[1] a conception repeated in the sun's descent into the black sea.

Satan's position on Job's right knee seems to be indicative of the fact that he is attacking Job's spiritual man. From " Jerusalem "[2] we may learn that the boils are probably to be regarded as each a " separate & deadly Sin," but they are such spiritual sins as " Doubt " and "Shame." Satan's weapons, the vial of flame and the darts, may be taken to be spiritual Sin and Death, as they are the insignia of Sin and Death (respectively), in the " Paradise Lost " designs.[3]

Job is henceforth naked, until, in Illustration 13, he is " clothed with the Divine mercy ! "[4]

The margin shows the potsherd[5] with which Job scraped himself (Job ii. 8), and his broken crook, telling of the passing of pastoral "Innocence." Above and around are a heaven and earth, in which only infernal and destructive creatures dwell.

---

[1] The head is normally the seat of spiritual " light," and the foot, of darkness. *Cp.* "thy immortal Head, in which Eternity dwells" ("Jm.", p. 86, l. 10; *cp.* " Jm.", p. 24, l. 10; " Mn.", p. 3, ll. 7, 8), etc., etc.

" May God who dwells in this dark Ulro & voidness, vengeance take,
    And draw thee down into this Abyss of sorrow and torture " ("Jm.", p 23, ll. 38-9).

Ulro is this life ("Jm", p. 44, ll. 21-2, etc.), and in a passage in " Mn.", it is used as equivalent to the foot (".Mn ", p. 19, ll. 4 *ff.*).

[2] "Jm.", p 21, ll. 4-5.

[3] The figures of Sin and Death (which first appear in his second design of the " Paradise Lost " series) are shown in the tenth, the former with vials belching flame, and the latter with darts (*vide* " Liverpool Booksellers" Edition). But *cp.* " Poetical Sketches," p. 62 : " The arrows of sin stick in my flesh." (" The Couch of Death," Sampson, p. 42).

[4] Letter to Thomas Butts, 10th Jan. 1802 (Russell, pp. 101-2).

[5] This broken vessel is probably symbolical of Job's " moral individuality." In Illustration 12, we see the last remnant of the potsherd thrown away under the feet of Elihu.
    Cp. ". . . . as the Potter breaks the potsherds ;
        Dashing in pieces Self-righteousnesses " ("Jm.", p. 78, ll. 5, 6).

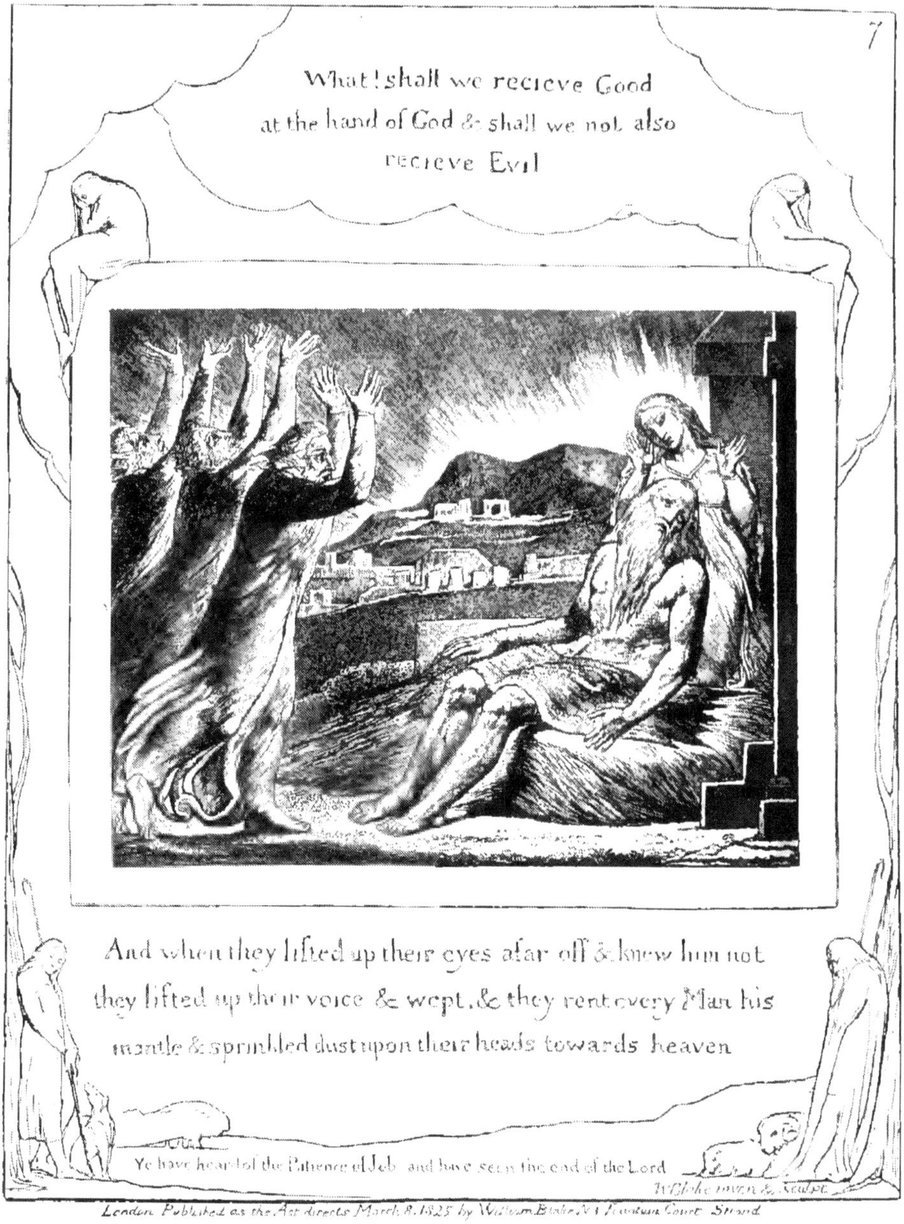
7
What! shall we recieve Good at the hand of God & shall we not also recieve Evil
And when they lifted up their eyes afar off & knew him not they lifted up their voice & wept, & they rent every Man his mantle & sprinkled dust upon their heads towards heaven
Ye have heard of the Patience of Job and have seen the end of the Lord
W Blake inven & sculpt
London Published as the Act directs March 8. 1825 by William Blake No 3 Fountain Court Strand

ILLUSTRATION VII

"Corporeal friends are spiritual enemies" ("Jm.", p. 30, l. 10).

"MERCY changd Death into Sleep."[1]   The margin here shows us four sleeping figures ; Job and his wife appearing below leaning peacefully asleep against supporting trees, in a gentle pastoral landscape.   For the moment, Job's personal heroism and patience has triumphed over all adversity, and we see the valley of experience in its milder aspect.   Even the horizon where his sun is deeply set, is lit with flashes of the Aurora or Northern Dawn.

If only he could have been left to himself it seems he might have endured, but that is just what he has to learn cannot be. As we have already seen (Illus. 5), it is useless "striving to Create a Heaven in which all shall be pure & holy in their Own Selfhoods."[2] Whether we like it or not, we live amongst men, and in times of trouble it is a part of "Christianity" to learn to receive even the ill-advised consolations of our friends.[3]   Blake himself had some-times found it harder to accept their sympathy than to endure

---

[1] Tirzah, v. 2, "S. of E."; cp. "The Sleep of Ulro" ("Jm.", p. 4, l. 1).

[2] "Jm.", p. 49, ll. 27-28.

[3] "It is easier to forgive an Enemy than to forgive a Friend:" ("Jm.", p. 91, l. 1); cp. Humourous epigram in MS. book (Sampson, p. 216).

> "Thy friendship oft has made my heart to ake :
> Do be my Enemy—for Friendship's sake."

Cp. "And in the midst of the Great Assembly Palamabron prayd:
O God protect me from my friends, that they have not power over me
Thou hast giv'n me power to protect myself from my bitterest enemies."

("Mn.", p. 7, ll. 4-6).

adversity itself.   He doubtless describes his own experience in the words—

> "To do unkind things in kindness ! with power armd, to say
> The most irritating things in the midst of tears and love
> These are the stings of the Serpent ! " [1]

And he reiterates the saying, "Corporeal Friends" (these friends as we see from the position of their feet are to be regarded as corporeal friends) "are Spiritual Enemies." [2]   There can be little doubt that Blake found in the silent sympathy of Job's friends the aggravating cause of his abrupt change from a sublime resignation to bitter despair ; from a frame of mind of which he says to his wife, "What ? shall we receive good at the hand of God and shall we not receive evil ?"—to that in which he breaks out in the words, "Let the day perish wherein I was born."   What is certain is that, for the next three designs, which lead us to the end of the descent, the place of Satan is taken by the three friends.

The masonry of Job's house, though still heavy and square-set, gives the suggestion of a cross. [3]

---

[1] " Mⁿ.", p. 10, ll. 32-34.

[2] " Mⁿ.", p. 3 (extra page), l. 26 (" Jᵐ.", p. 30, l. 10) ; and *cp.* " Jᵐ.", p. 91, ll. 15, 16, and also letter to Thomas Butts, 25th April 1803 (Russell, pp. 114, 115).

[3] *I am glad to find this observation confirmed in Mr Charles Eliot Norton's book, written in America in 1875 (Boston, Osgood & Co.), but unfortunately not seen by me till my book was in the press.   Mr Norton also notes the cross in Illus. 10, and with needless modesty suggests the true meaning of the "pagan cairns." He is also, I believe, the only editor to note both the sunset and sunrise " As it was sunset in the opening scene, it is sunrise now," he says in his commentary to Plate XXi.*

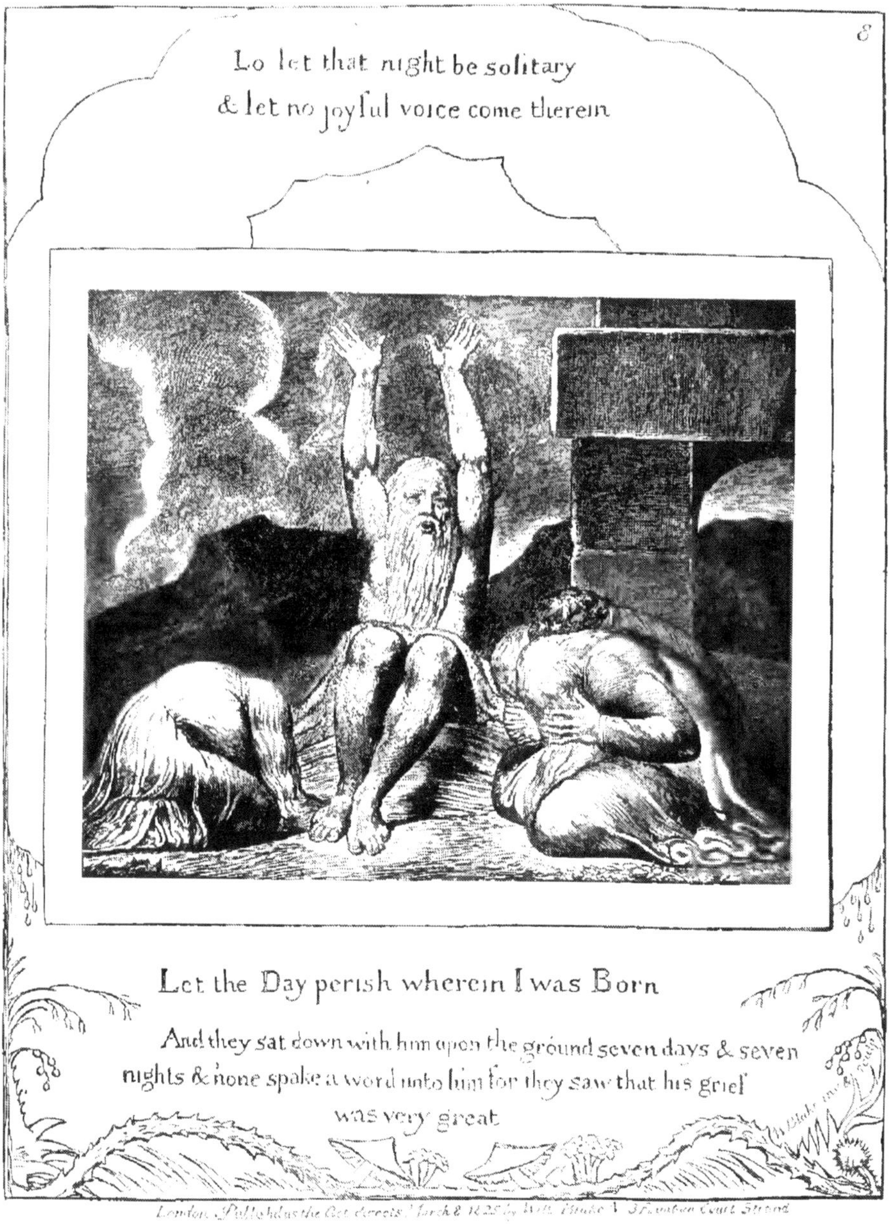
8
Lo let that night be solitary
& let no joyful voice come therein
Let the Day perish wherein I was Born
And they sat down with him upon the ground seven days & seven nights & none spake a word unto him for they saw that his grief was very great

London. Publishd as the Act directs March 8 1825 by Will Blake No 3 Fountain Court Strand

ILLUSTRATION VIII

"It is an easy thing to talk of patience to the afflicted" (" F. Z.").

THIS design shows us Job's defeat. Job cursed his day and said, "Let that night be solitary," and "Let the Day perish wherein I was Born." The story, as we find it in the Bible, offers no explanation of this sudden surrender to despair, and modern Biblical criticism being unknown in Blake's days, he could not account for the want of continuity by the theory that the first two chapters in prose are an introduction added later to the ancient poem.[1] The Illustration is, therefore, an instance of Blake's finding and bringing out his own continuity, which he discovers in the sympathy of the friends ; making it the aggravating cause of Job's outburst.[2]

Again we have the tremendous effect of the landscape in emphasising Job's distress, and the sense of unyielding oppression in the masonry behind the three friends on Job's left. Their "religion" is harsh and inhuman like poor Job's own, while unlike his, it is not redeemed by their practice, nor softened by personal suffering.

The margin shows heavy clouds weeping upon thorns, weeds and funguses.

[1] "There is a contradiction, therefore, between the introduction, in which he is represented as eminently patient, and the dialogues that follow, in which he indulges in passionate complaints and accusations of God. This contradiction is so marked as to induce many scholars to reject the introduction as a later addition. . ." Prof. Oort ("Bible for Young People," tr. by Philip H. Wicksteed, vol. iv. chap. xiv. p. 164).

[2] Vide supra, pp. 75-6.

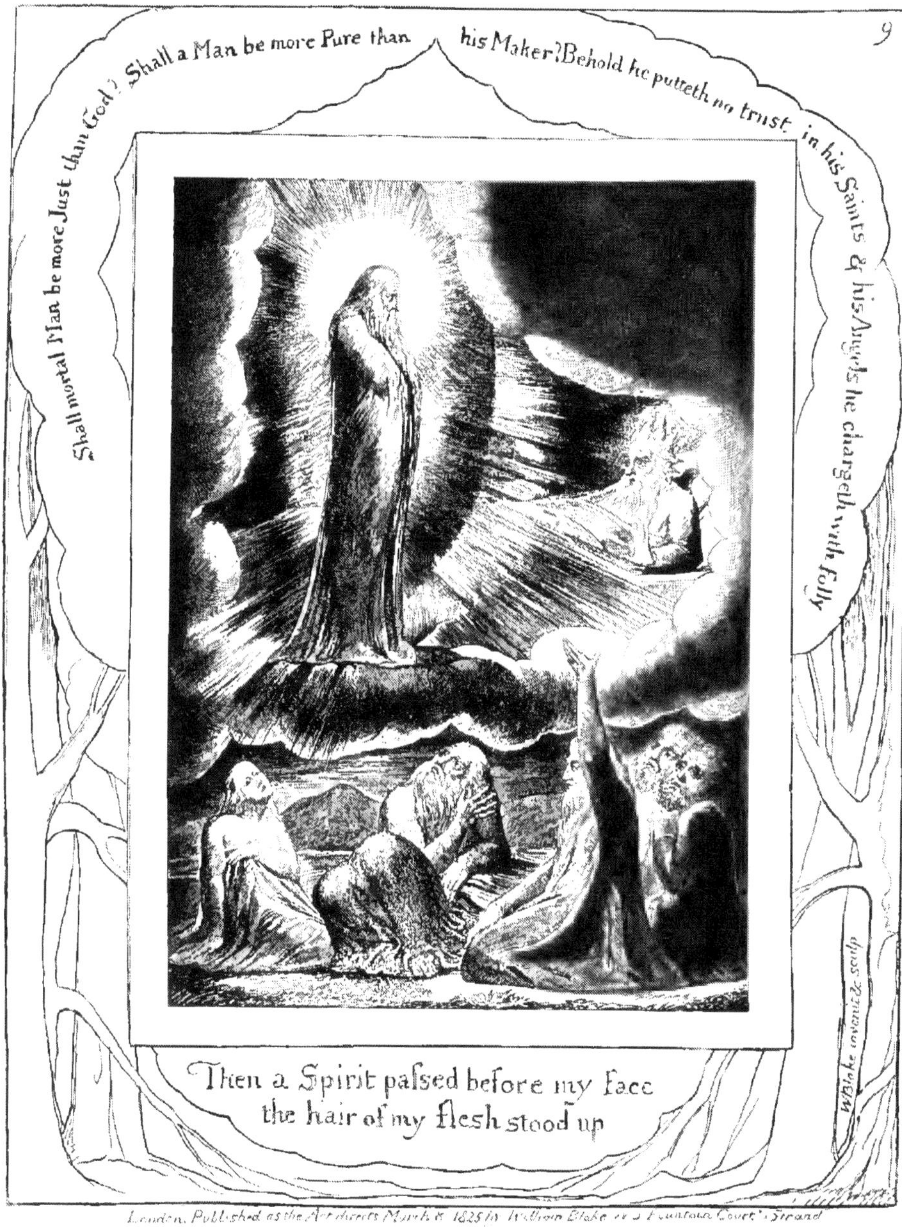
9
Shall mortal Man be more Just than God? Shall a Man be more Pure than his Maker? Behold he putteth no trust in his Saints & his Angels he chargeth with folly
Then a Spirit pafsed before my face
the hair of my flesh stood up
WBlake invenit & sculp

London, Published as the Act directs March 8 1825 by William Blake No 3 Fountain Court Strand

ILLUSTRATION IX

" All Love is lost ! terror succeeds & Hatred instead of Love
And stern demands of Right & Duty, instead of Liberty "
(" J^m.", p. 22, ll. 10, 11 ; also " F. Z.").
"God out of Christ is a Consuming Fire."
Legend on Allegorical Painting (now in Tate Gallery).

THIS marvellous Invention represents Eliphaz rebuking Job by revealing his own vision of Deity. All except Eliphaz look up at it as something outside themselves. For him alone it is within, an aspect of his own mind and life. And as the Deity was before represented in the likeness of Job, being Job's inmost self, so this Deity is in the likeness of Eliphaz. It is significant that of the earthly man the left side only is shown in the design, whereas it is his Divine-man's right side that we see. The dreaming form above is again the earthly man, smitten with deadly terror at the vision of his own spiritual being. His God is not the God of love, nor the God of life and action ; for his brow is stern and his arms are bound about him. Before him no creature can be justified. "Behold he putteth no trust in his Saints," as the text in the margin says, "& he chargeth his Angels with folly." Light flashes from his whole figure, but, like the spirit itself, it is fierce and comfortless.

The design is the counterpart of the one in Job's ascent (Illus. 17), where the human Deity appears in the form of Christ putting Job's friends to shame.

The margin is filled with heavy cloud and trees that bear no fruit or foliage.

79

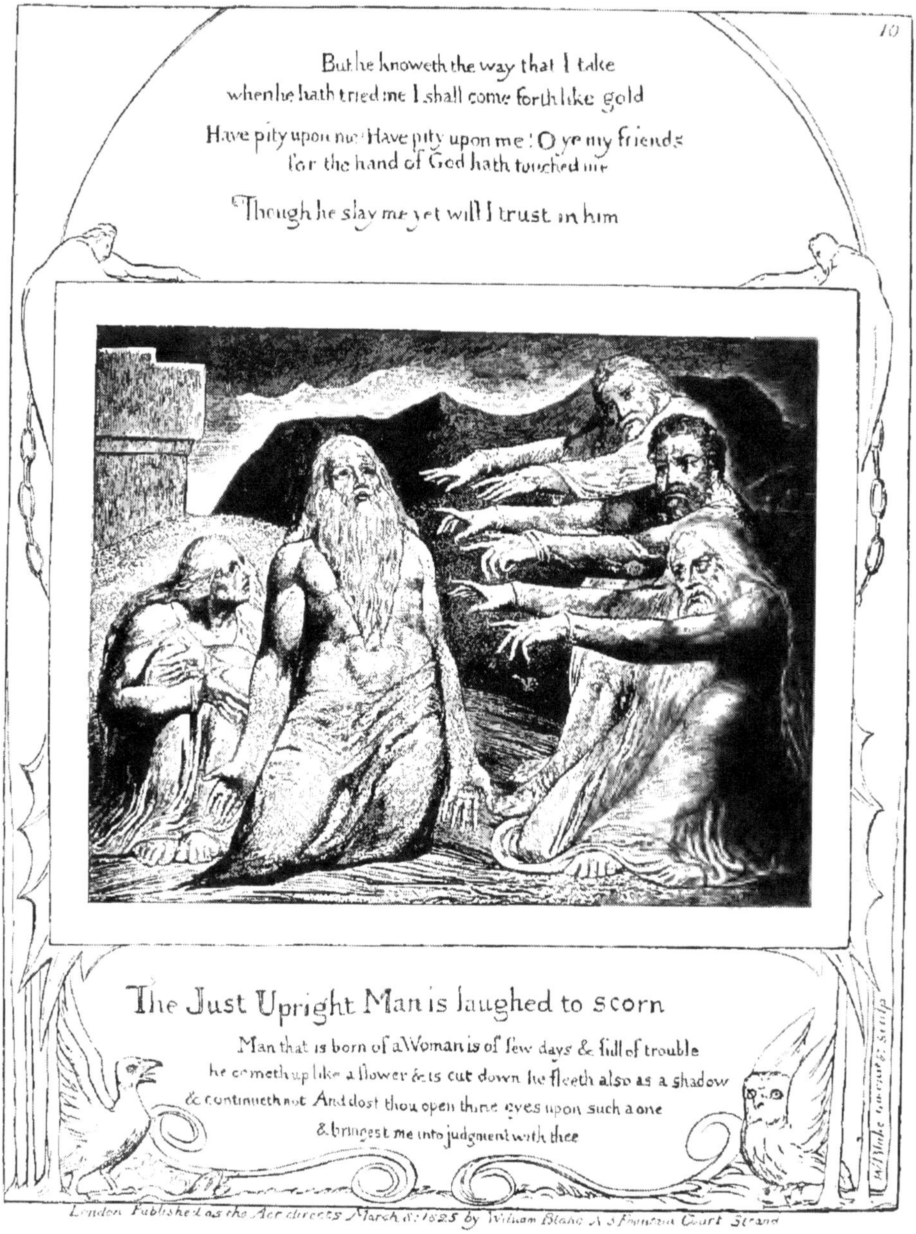
10
But he knoweth the way that I take
when he hath tried me I shall come forth like gold
Have pity upon me! Have pity upon me! O ye my friends
for the hand of God hath touched me
Though he slay me yet will I trust in him
The Just Upright Man is laughed to scorn
Man that is born of a Woman is of few days & full of trouble
he cometh up like a flower & is cut down he fleeth also as a shadow
& continueth not And dost thou open thine eyes upon such a one
& bringest me into judgment with thee
London Published as the Act directs March 8: 1825 by William Blake N 3 Fountain Court Strand

ILLUSTRATION X

" . . . however loving
And merciful the Individuality; however high
Our palaces, and cities, and however fruitful are our fields
In Selfhood, we are nothing; but fade away in mornings breath " (" Jᵐ.", p. 45, ll. 10-13).

GOADED to desperation by the inhuman conception of Deity shown him by Eliphaz, whose God affords no hope of justification for any living thing, Job makes appeal to his own vision of God; the terrible answer to which we shall see in the next Illustration.

For a man like Job there is only one way of salvation, though for weaker spirits there may be an easier way, as we shall see in Illustration 18. Job must go through with his error to the bitter end,[1] until actual experience has broken it in his hand. A man of less heroic calibre, or, as Blake would say, of less "intellect,"[2] would have conceded his guilt before he had learnt to understand his error. But Job knows that, according to his lights, he has been scrupulously faithful. And it is by holding fast to this truth, that he comes at last to see that his light itself was darkness.

The symbolic significance of the hands and feet in this design is curious and somewhat elaborate, but cannot be neglected because of the interest of the chapter in Blake's thought, to which it directs attention. It will be noticed that the friends, who are full of angry scorn, rise one behind the other in a kind of ascending scale. Each of them extends both hands, though the right hands are a little

[1] "If the fool would persist in his folly he would become wise" ("M. H. H.," p. 7). "The road of excess leads to the palace of wisdom" (*Ibid.*). "No man can embrace true art till he has explored and cast out false art." "V. L. J." (Gilchrist, ii. p. 195), etc.; *cp.* note 4, Preface, p. 21.
[2] "The treasures of heaven are not negations of passion, but realities of intellect. . . . The fool shall not enter into heaven, let him be ever so holy." "V. L. J." (Gilchrist, ii. p. 197).

more advanced.   And though each shows only one foot, taken as a
group they show both ; again, with a preponderance of right (two
right to one left), Job's wife shows her right hand before her left
and both feet, the right one again being slightly more advanced ;
while Job himself shows neither foot.

Now, if we admit Blake's use of symbolism in the hands and
feet at all, it is not to be supposed that he meant nothing in
particular by this arrangement.   And a little investigation into his
general conceptions reveals certain thoughts connected with the
error of self-righteousness, which might very well be indicated by
this marshalling of all the forces of spiritual and corporeal denuncia-
·tion against poor Job's conviction of innocence.   For the man who
pleads his own righteousness shows that he entirely fails to understand
the nature of the body and the bodily life, and, *still more*, that he fails
to understand the nature of the spirit and the spiritual life.   The
bodily life, Blake thinks, is incapable of right as such,[1] and the law
of corporeal, or external righteousness, is inherently monstrous.[2]

For the bodily life is the life of separation in which we illusively
appear to be divided from our fellow-men.[3]   And the supreme good

[1] " Man is born a Spectre or Satan & is altogether an Evil, & requires a New Selfhood continually " ("J^m.", p. 52).   " The Selfish Virtues of the Natural Heart." (*Ibid.*).
    " No individual can keep these Laws, for they are death to every energy of man,
and forbid the springs of life : " (" J^m.", p. 35, ll. 11, 12).
    [2] " Natural Morality or Self-Righteousness " (" J^m.," p. 52).
    " Self-righteousnesses conglomerating against the Divine Vision : " (" J^m.",
p. 13, l. 52).
    " Satan . . . to pervert the Divine voice in its entrance to the earth . . . Saying
I am God alone there is no other : let all obey my principles of moral individuality "
("Mⁿ.", p. 7, ll. 19-26).
    [3] " Albion," in his evil dreams of night, condemns the " labours of loves," and
makes " solid rocks " of " demonstrative truth," in order " that Man be separate from
Man " (" J^m.", p. 28, ll. 5-12), etc.
    Cp. " J^m.", p. 31, ll. 7-10, etc., where " Albion " (that is Humanity, *vide*

ILLUSTRATION X   83

being a spiritual or poetic identification of ourselves with others,[1] is the contrary of the bodily life. And, in the same way, the life of the spirit being the life of universal union, it is clearly impossible that spiritual righteousness should be attributed to separate individuals. We may take our choice, but we cannot have both. We can either shut ourselves up in our own physical individuality, in which case we are not righteous ; or we may enter the universal Spiritual life, in which case our righteousness is not our own private property. But we cannot at the same time remain units, and accredit those units with what only belongs to the whole as a whole.

The case of a good man such as Job being enslaved by this error, is beautifully expressed in a passage in " Jerusalem " :—

> " The Man is himself become
> A piteous example of oblivion. To teach the Sons
> Of Eden, that however great and glorious ; however loving
> And merciful the Individuality ; however high
> Our palaces and cities, and however fruitful are our fields
> In Selfhood, we are nothing ; but fade away in mornings breath.
> Our mildness is nothing : the greatest mildness we can use
> Is incapable and nothing : none but the Lamb of God can heal
> This dread disease : none but Jesus : O Lord ! descend and save ! "
> ("Jᵐ.", p. 45, ll. 8-16.)

---

list of verbal emendations to "Vala," where Blake often changes "Man" to "Albion" in revising, cp. E. & Y., iii., "Vala," pp. 149-168, especially "Night," iii. p. 152), is divided into parts, each of which take up "the articulations of a mans soul," and Los finds these "hidden within in the minute particulars of which they had possessd themselves."

[1] " When in Eternity Man converses with Man they enter
    Into each others Bosom (which are Universes of delight) "
    ("Jᵐ.", p. 88, ll. 3-4).

" Every kindness to another is a little Death in the Divine Image nor can Man exist but by Brotherhood" ("Jᵐ.", p. 96, ll. 27-28).

" To give his vegetated body to be cut off & separated that the Spiritual body may be reveald " (" F. Z.," cp. "Vala," viii. ll. 261-2).

In a later Illustration we shall see how Jesus—that is to say, the Universal Humanity in Blake's system—redeems both Job and his friends. Meanwhile the friends are right in what they say—it is their attitude of condemnation and scorn that is wrong. In accusing Job they "punish the already punish'd,"[1] and are guilty of the one error greater than Job's own. For the only thing Blake seems to think worse than attributing righteousness to ourselves, is attributing sin to others.

Job's wife is nearest the truth, though she, too, is dominated by a cross of stone.[2] Her attitude is intellectually the same, but emotionally the opposite of that of the friends. To them, Job's error is a subject for angry accusation. To her, it is a subject for passionate sympathy, for while she justly expostulates with him, she weeps for him at the same time.

The little flower visible beneath Eliphaz' left hand, and the marginal text referring to it, should be noticed. They remind us of the pathetic side there is to this obstinate attempt of men to be saved in their own right. For regarded as a unit, what is man better than a flower that "cometh up" and is "cut down"? "In Selfhood we are nothing; but fade away in mornings breath."

The lower margin shows us birds of prey whose life is maintained at the expense of others.[3] The things like thin trees are probably not trees at all, but down-descending "tubes," some of

---

[1] "J^m", p. 31, l. 34; cp. "J^m.", p. 77, ll. 26-28 (of poem).

[2] *Vide* final note, Illus. 7, p. 76.

[3] The necessity of the preying of life on life is sometimes put by Blake into the mouths of his fallen or diabolical personations, apparently representing the supreme cynicism ("J^m.", p. 42, l. 49).

"F. Z ," cp. "Vala," vii. l. 385:

> "That life lives upon death, and by devouring appetite
> All things subsist on one another."

ILLUSTRATION X   85

them apparently springing from the sharp-edged wings of the Fiend. They speak of the division of the divine-life into the separate forms of earth. "I sunk with cries of blood . . . rolling in tubelike forms shut up within themselves descending down."[1]

Blake's meaning expressed in the texts and symbolism of the upper margin is very interesting and leads on to the next design, but can only be understood with reference to his doctrine of error. Error is ultimately no less redemptive than truth, but its way is through the Purgatory of failure, pain and horror. One cannot doubt that in quoting the first of the marginal texts Blake had in mind the two preceding verses also : "Behold, I go forward, but he is not there ; and backward, but I cannot perceive him : on the left hand, where he doth work, but I cannot behold him : he hideth himself on the right hand, that I cannot see him."[2] Job now fully realises that God is against him on every side, corporeal and spiritual alike, but his faith suffers no diminution. "Though he slay me," he says, "yet will I trust in him." And this faith indeed saves him ; but not from being slain. On the contrary it is only through his spiritual destruction that the way is made ready in his soul for the redeeming light. He must die in order to live. Yet his error, personified in the next Illustration as his Satanic Selfhood, is in a sense the vehicle of the Eternal Mercy, for it too serves the great end of redemption. "Come Lord Jesus," Blake says in "Jerusalem," "take on thee the Satanic Body of Holiness."[3] And to some extent every man must take on the Satanic body in some form, therein enduring its inevitable cross of suffering, before he can finally win his eternal liberty.

[1] "F. Z." cp. "Vala," vii. ll. 284-6.
[2] Job xxiii. vv. 8, 9.
[3] "Jm.", p. 90, l. 38.

The strange bow (if it is a bow) bent above, and the chain falling below, may very probably be taken to symbolise the two aspects of Satan's " principles of moral individuality." Job's faith in individual duty and self-constraint, rather than in liberty guided by a passionate love of all mankind, would thus be symbolised by the tightly sprung bow; the friends' error of coercive and penalising law by the chain.[1] Job is to learn in the horror of the coming vision that his religion is the same as that of his friends, against which he has appealed. He learns charity to them at the same time that his own infernal error burns itself out of his soul.

---

[1] The grounds for the above suggested interpretation are of several kinds. The chain is sufficiently obvious, in itself and in its meaning   But the probability that the arch above represents a bow, is derived from such a passage as—

> " A bended bow is lifted in heaven, & a heavy iron chain
> Descends link by link from Albions cliffs across the sea to bind
> Brothers & sons of America," (" America," p. 3, ll 7-9).

The suggestion that the bow represents restraint comes from the corner figures who punctuate (perhaps even personate) the two ends of the bow. They appear to be clinging on to the square frame, and thus resisting the bow's outward spring, and, what is even more significant, their hands are draped in their gowns, which recalls the arm-bound figure of the Deity as he appeared to Eliphaz in the previous Illustration (Illus. 9), and almost certainly speaks of the righteousness of prohibitions, with its deadly curbing of the active life.

So far the weakest point is the character of the bow   But I am afraid one must suspect Blake of associating the ring formed by the bow and chain with the diurnal solar cycle.   This destroys the bow as a " bended bow," but accounts for its spreading as it descends and for the figure on the spectators' left (dayspring), being a youth, while the one on his right (nightfall) is more aged.   The descending chain is certainly frequently associated with Los and the Time-process (" Urizen," ch. vii. vv. 2, 3, p. 18; and " Jm.", p. 11, ll. 1, 2 ; cp. Illus , " Urizen," p. 19; " Jm.", p. 6). The association of the bow with Satan and the Moral law occurs again in the poem (" Jm.", p. 52):—

> " When Satan first the black bow bent
> And the Moral Law from the Gospel rent "
>
>   (" Jm.," p. 52 ; Poem, v. 5).

11

My bones are pierced in me in the
night season & my sinews
take no rest

My skin is black upon me
& my bones are burned
with heat

The triumphing of the wicked
is short, the joy of the hypocrite is
but for a moment

Satan himself is transformed into an Angel of Light & his Ministers into Ministers of Righteousness

With Dreams upon my bed thou scarest me & affrightest me
with Visions

Why do you persecute me as God & are not satisfied with my flesh. Oh that my words
were printed in a Book that they were graven with an iron pen & lead in the rock for ever
For I know that my Redeemer liveth & that he shall stand in the latter days upon
the Earth & after my skin destroy thou This body yet in my flesh shall I see God
whom I shall see for Myself and mine eyes shall behold & not Another the consumed be my wrought image

Who opposeth & exalteth himself above all that is called God or is Worshipped

W Blake invent & sculp

London Published as the Act directs March 8. 1825 by Will Blake N 3 Fountain Court Strand

ILLUSTRATION XI

" Cloth'd in the Serpents folds, in selfish holiness demanding purity" ("Mᴰ.", p. 10, l. 46).

HERE we reach the bottom of the pit. Lying upon his narrow bed in utter isolation from all human fellowship, Job becomes a prey to the hideous phantoms of his own spiritual creed, and the God he has been worshipping appears in response to his appeal. Job looks down terrified at the flames of hell into which demons are dragging him, and holding up chains ready to bind him fast. Above is the still more horrible form of his Deity, whom he tries to hold off. The alternatives to which this Being points are both unutterable hell, though the one to which his right hand points purports to be heaven. For Blake says in his notes to Lavater's "Aphorisms," "Hell is the being shut up in the possession of corporeal desires,"[1] this is the obvious and flaming hell below. But in his "Vision of the Last Judgment," he says: "In Hell, all is self-righteousness"[2] and this is the hell above, where the two rounded stones represent the tables of the prohibitive law ; the ideal of which is the punishment of sin, rather than the liberation of man's passion for love and beauty out of which all human good is born.[3] The Deity who

---

[1] " Lav.," 299 (Ellis, p. 133). The whole note is as follows :—" To hell till he behaves better, mark that I do not believe there is such a thing literally, but hell is the being shut up in the possession of corporeal desires which shortly weary the man, FOR ALL LIFE IS HOLY."

[2] Gilchrist, ii. p. 199.

[3] " The tables of stone which utter lightning," *vide* " The design of the Last Judgment" (first description as given in J. T. Smith's Biographical Sketch " Letter to Ozias Humphrey." Symons, p. 383); *cp.* " Garden of Love," " S. of E.," " Gates of Paradise " [Prologue], etc., etc.

87

offers this horrible alternative is actually Satan, as we see by the cloven hoof of his left leg.[1]   But he is Satan in the likeness of Job; he is, in fact, the Great Selfhood worshipped as God.   Coiled round him and following his left arm is the Serpent,[2] who symbolises Nature[3] as opposed to Art and the regenerate life.[4]   It is Nature in this aspect that enforces Satan's alternative—the Hell of sensuality or the Hell of self-righteousness—both individualistic and hostile to the deeper humanity.

The marginal texts are important.   The first two (in the corners) are strictly in place in the story, and may even at one time have suggested the design.   The third (above in centre) is from a speech of Zopha's : " The triumphing of the wicked is short, and the joy of the hypocrite but for a moment."   In a sense, no doubt, this refers to poor Job, as Zopha of course intended.   But it is rather to his Satanic and slanderous Self[5] as represented here by the evil Deity, than to his eternal and true identity.   The fourth, " Satan himself is transformed into an Angel of Light and his Ministers into Ministers of Righteousness," is taken from the Epistles, slightly modified (2 Cor. xi. 14-15).   Blake, as we have already seen, believes that we make a religion out of our most profoundly selfish instincts, and he uses the text to express what he says to the " Deists," in " Jerusalem " (p. 52): " Man must & will have Some Religion : if he has not the Religion of Jesus, he will have the

---

[1] " Where Satan making to himself Laws from his own identity,
  Compell'd others to serve him in moral gratitude & submission
  Being call'd God ; setting himself above all that is called God."
  ("Mⁿ.", p. 9, ll. 10-12.)

[2] " Mⁿ.", p. 10, ll. 46-7 ; cp. Job xxvi. 13.

[3] " F. Z.," " Vala," iii. ll. 97 and 101 ; " Jm.", p. 29, ll. 76 and 80, etc.

[4] " [Satan] calls the Individual Law, Holy : and despises the Saviour." ("Mⁿ.", p. 11, l. 5).

[5] Vide supra note 4, p. 52.

ILLUSTRATION XI 89

Religion of Satan, & will erect the Synagogue of Satan, calling the Prince of this World, God ; and destroying all who do not worship Satan under the Name of God." The text immediately below the design is compiled from Job vii. 13-14. The longer one beneath is nearly the same as Job xix. 22-27, until we come to the last sentence, where Blake alters "though my reins be consumed within me" of the Bible to (presumably his own) "Tho consumed be my wrought Image." This suggests that Job is now learning the insignificance of his personal life as being merely the "wrought image" of his own eternal being. Another significant alteration is the change of "*worms destroy this body*" into "destroy *thou* this body." The *thou*, refers no doubt, to Nature as the Satanic power,[1] which is sometimes symbolised by the serpent and sometimes (especially man's mortal nature) by a worm.[2] From this abyss of horror Job is aroused by the wrath of Elihu.

[1] "*Cp.* "H. C. R. Diary," "Nature is the work of the Devil," 24th Dec. 1825 (Symons, p. 265).
[2] "F. Z.," "Vala," ix. l. 624, etc. ; *cp.* "Urizen," chap. vi. v. 5, "The worm lay till it grew to a serpent."

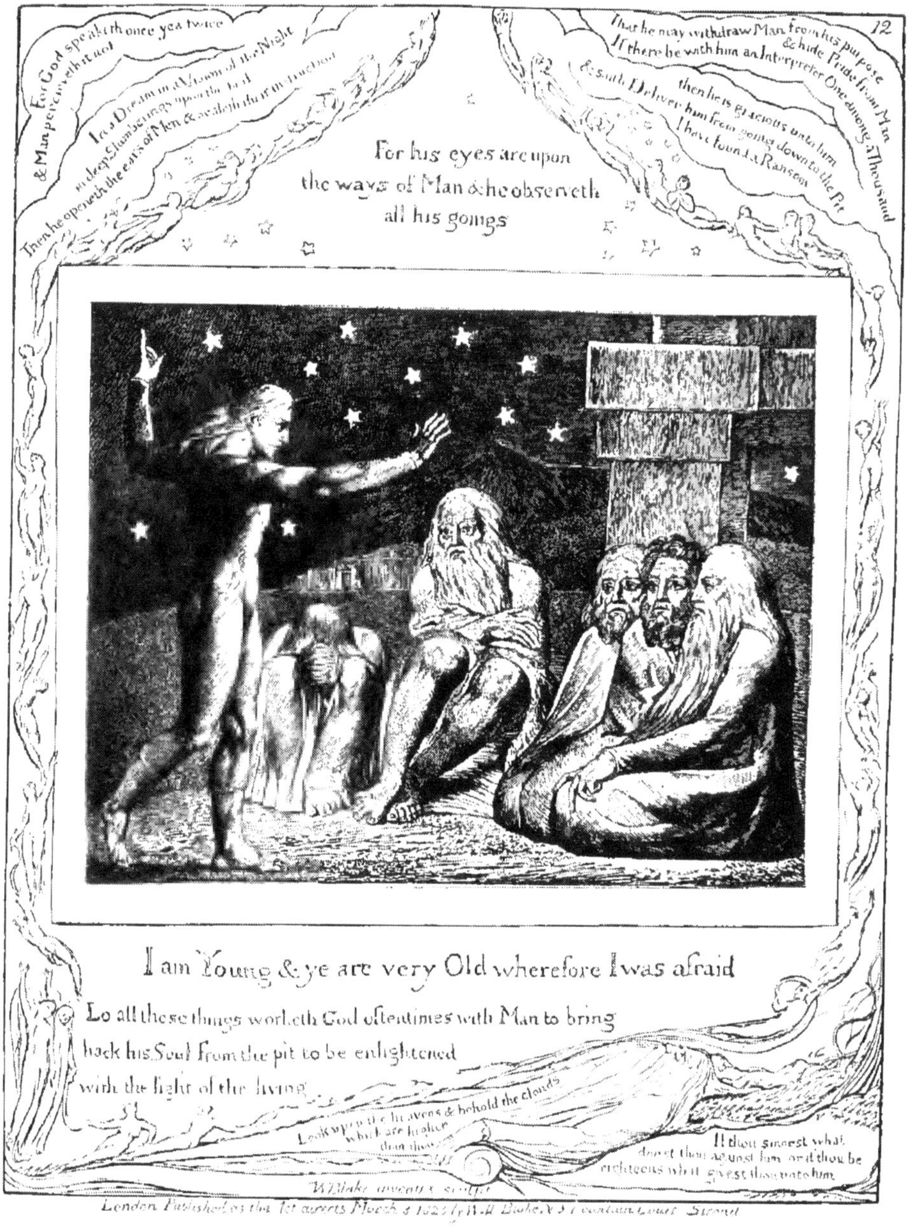
12
For God speaketh once yea twice
& Man perceiveth it not
In a Dream in a Vision of the Night
in deep Slumberings upon the bed
Then he openeth the ears of Men & sealeth their instruction
That he may withdraw Man from his purpose
& hide Pride from Man
If there be with him an Interpreter One among a Thousand
then he is gracious unto him
& saith Deliver him from going down to the Pit
I have found a Ransom
For his eyes are upon
the ways of Man & he observeth
all his goings
I am Young & ye are very Old wherefore I was afraid
Lo all these things worketh God oftentimes with Man to bring
back his Soul from the pit to be enlightened
with the light of the living
Look upon the heavens & behold the clouds
which are higher
than thou
If thou sinnest what
doest thou against him or if thou be
righteous what givest thou unto him
W Blake invenit & sculpsit
London Published as the Act directs March 8 1825 by W Blake No 3 Fountain Court Strand

ILLUSTRATION XII

" Thus were the stars of heaven created like a golden chain
To bind the Body of Man to heaven from falling into the abyss" ("F Z ")

THE spirit of the marginal design here shows that the crisis is past. In place of the fierce flames of the preceding page, we see Job sleeping peacefully "in a Dream," as the marginal text says, "in a Vision of the Night, in deep Slumberings, upon the bed,"—and from his body hosts of happy spirits are seen to soar up to the stars.

In the main design, Elihu appears and undertakes to speak on behalf of God to whom Job has appealed. But though he speaks for Deity he expressly claims his own mere humanity. " Behold I am according to thy wish in God's stead ; I also am formed out of the clay "[1] : a passage which Blake does not quote, but symbolises by showing Elihu with left foot forward. But though Elihu is thus expressly represented as "corporeal," he is not necessarily a "spiritual enemy," like the other "friends," for unlike them he comes in wrath. And Blake says, "The man may be the friend of my spiritual life while he seems the enemy of my corporeal, though not *vice versa*."[2] Elihu comes to rebuke and to chastise the corporeal man. God's intent, he says, is to "withdraw Man from his purpose & hide Pride from Man." And for Blake this text doubtless speaks of the pride and purposes of self-righteousness ; the great corporeal error of Job and his friends.

The keynote of the Illustration is clearly struck by the stars ; both the twelve great luminaries to which Elihu points in the main design, and those to which the marginal spirits ascend. But here a difficulty occurs. Elihu, whose intervention is the whole theme of the Illustration, does not once mention the stars ; and Blake's

[1] Job xxxiii. 6.
[2] Letter to Thos. Butts, 25th April 1803 (Russell, pp. 114-5).

91

marginal texts, which are exclusively from Elihu's speech, refer only to the heavens and the clouds.[1]

What then did the stars symbolise for Blake that he should go out of his way to give them so critical a place in the development of his story of Job?

In the first place, I cannot doubt that they are intended to emphasise the depth of night which Job's soul has now reached. For him the only heavens remaining are the heavens of night; and if Elihu points him to the skies, he will see no light in these except such as the night itself affords. This is, in fact, that darkest hour which comes before the dawn, but which for that very reason is the most resplendent with the stars.

But a hint of something more deeply significant is given by the spirits emanating from Job's sleeping body in the margin. These are unquestionably what Blake calls "emanations," and he says, "Man is adjoind to Man by his Emanative portion."[2] Here the emanations adjoin Job to the stars, and it seems not improbable, therefore, that just as the sun is the symbol of Job's own inner spirit (either as the halo of Deity, or rising and setting on the horizon), so the stars may be the souls of other men, as distantly perceived by him across the abyss of nature, which in this corporeal life separates man from man.[3] The marginal spirits at all events are

[1] The use of the marginal texts in this design has already been explained in the Introduction (note 4, p. 41, q.v.).

[2] "Jm.", p. 44, l. 38; cp. "Jm.", p. 88, l. 10.

[3] "Shuddering
With their wings they sat in the Furnace, in a night
Of stars, for all the Sons of Albion appeard distant stars.
Ascending and descending into Albions sea of death."
("Jm.", p. 50, ll. 18-21.)

Cp. "F. Z.," "Howling & Wailing fly the souls from Urizen's strong hand,
For from the hand of Urizen the myriads fall like stars"
("Vala," ix. ll. 321, 322).

ILLUSTRATION XII 93

Job's "emanative portion," taking him out of his self-centred world and joining him with the spirits of other life in the universe. "Lo, all these things worketh God oftentimes with Man," says Elihu in the margin, "to bring back his Soul from the pit, to be enlightened with the light of the living."

A closer study of the marginal design yields some interesting further suggestions, which tend to show that Blake still adhered in his old age to the position set forth in "The Marriage of Heaven and Hell" as to the divine character of the body; though we must never forget that even there it is the body regarded as "a portion of Soul."[1] In his "Vision of the Last Judgment" he says that "in Paradise they have no corporeal and mortal body," yet this must be read in the light of the previous sentence where he says that it is possible to "live in Paradise and Liberty . . . in spirit, but not in the mortal body . . . *till after a Last Judgment*,"[2] but he also says in the same work, "Whenever any individual rejects error, and embraces truth, a Last Judgment passes upon that individual."[3]

This clearly suggests that we may live in Paradise, *even in the body*, when we have rejected error. Which suggestion is abundantly confirmed by much that Blake wrote in his earlier days. In his notes to Swedenborg's "Angelic Wisdom," he says, referring to a passage about keeping the understanding in spiritual light, "This, Man can do while in the body."[4] To another passage where Swedenborg says, "Man, in whom the spiritual Degree is open, comes into that Wisdom when he dies, and may also come into it by laying asleep the Sensations of the Body," Blake points the moral by

[1] "M. H. H.," p. 4.
[2] "V. L. J.," Gilchrist, ii. p. 198 (italics mine).
[3] *Ibid.*, Gilchrist, ii. p. 196.   [4] "Swed.," p. 33.

saying, "This is while in the Body," and also, "This is to be understood as unusual in our time but common in ancient."[1]

In his notes to Lavater's "Aphorisms," he says, "Man is a twofold being, one part capable of evil and the other capable of good. That which is capable of good is not also capable of evil, but that which is capable of evil is also capable of good."[2]—And though he does not elsewhere always admit the twofold character of man, yet that is because when the evil element or aspect of that "part capable of evil" has been rejected (as it is by a "Last Judgment"), then the two parts are indeed one; "heaven and hell," in fact, are married.[3]

It is a kindred idea which here seems to be treated in the margin. We see the stars approached by two streams of spirits ascending from Job's sleeping body; the one from his head and the other from his feet. The former rises straight up unaided, but the latter lie in deep sleep upon his lower man until gradually roused and wakened by the guiding angels, who hold them out a scroll and direct them up towards heaven. This suggests that the expressions or emanations, even of our lower or corporeal being, are capable of "adjoining man to man" when enlightened. And that once awakened they may link us with the same heavens as our spiritual ideas do.

This again connects itself with the very clear indications that the *stars*, whatever else they may symbolise, are the point of contact between the spiritual and the corporeal visions of life, or the irreducible minimum of spiritual reality which even the corporeal vision cannot quench; the fragments of universal light which Night itself cannot drown. "Thus were the stars of heaven

---

[1] "Swed.," p. 220.   [2] "Lav.," 479 (Ellis, p. 141).
[3] This subject is further treated in Illus. 18.

ILLUSTRATION XII   95

created like a golden chain To bind the Body of Man to heaven from falling into the abyss." [1]   In " Jerusalem " he says that " Los reads the Stars," Los being the prophetic spirit labouring in this life to preserve the divine vision,[2] whereas his " Spectre," the rationalising and materialistic power in Man [3] " reads the Voids between the Stars."[4]   The point of the contrast being that to both, the actual appearance is the same ; it is in the reading of it that the difference appears.   Los and the Spectre both represent corporeal truth,[2] the one enlightened and the other dark.[5]

But now once more to examine the minutiæ of the marginal design.   We see that there are actually two streams of emanations moving each way.   From the scroll in Job's left hand proceed certain dim unformed figures that are finally lost in the current

[1] " F. Z.," *cp.* " Vala," ii. ll. 266-7
[2] " Jᵐ.", p. 44, ll.28-31 ; " Mⁿ.", p. 23, l. 71, and " Jᵐ.", p. 95, ll. 17-20 (where, however, Los himself is relatively to his eternal Zoa, a Spectre).
[3] " Jᵐ.", p. 10, ll. 7-16, etc., etc.
[4] " Jᵐ.", p. 91, ll. 36, 7.
[5] There is an interesting passage in the " Milton " which further supports this idea of the stars being the point of contact between the illusory material universe and the true spiritual one.
In this passage the stars seem to be equated with " the Substances of Creation," in contrast to the " Newtonian Voids between " (" Mⁿ.", p. 37, l. 46):—

" For the Chaotic Voids outside of the Stars are measured by
The Stars, which are the boundaries of Kingdoms, Provinces
And Empires of Chaos invisible to the Vegetable Man."
(" Mⁿ.", p. 37, ll. 47-49.)

(The reason why they are invisible to the " Vegetable Man," though not to his " Reasoning Power," or " Spectre," is explained at the end of the passage from the " Milton " quoted note on p. 100, " As to that false appearance, etc.")
The difficulty of fixing the meaning of the stars with certainty is to find any passage where Blake says in unequivocal language what they signify.   It cannot, however, be doubted, I think, that their meaning must at all events include the one here attributed to them.   In three passages in " V. L. J." they are associated with children, representing nations or generations (Gilchrist, ii. pp. 188, 191, 192).

near the point where the higher stream is rescued by the angels. Again from Job's hair proceeds a stream which appears to be consumed in hot flames, kindled by veins of fire, some of which issue from the scroll. The soaring spirits above them proceed, not actually from Job's head but from a scroll that issues from his right side. Apparently, therefore, both our spiritual and corporeal emanations have their higher and lower forms. Those from the right-hand scroll are highest, those from the left-hand scroll are lowest. But from the lower man proceed redeemable and potentially vital and beautiful spirits, just as from the higher man proceed "brands" fit only for the burning.

If, therefore, the stars are what we have supposed, the reading of the design becomes clear. Once grasp the supreme reality of other lives in the universe, it then becomes a matter of secondary importance whether we are "in the body" or delivered from it. Once recognise that the supremely significant points in a material universe are the human spirits (which includes for Blake every creature and thing) which it embodies and environs, heaven is still within our grasp. On the other hand, a spiritual faith which is shut up in ideas of the importance and possibility of saving our individual souls, cuts us off from the greater universe, in which is the true life of all humanity. Job's spiritual individualism or self-righteousness is symbolised by the potsherd, the last remnant of which we see here thrown away beneath the feet of Elihu.[1]

Job's wife is still in the pit of despair, for this gospel of finding our good in the joy of others, brings little comfort to poor earthly grief, and the thought of a multitudinous life in the earth and heaven beyond, does not restore to her her own lost children. But we shall see her, too, uplifted in the following design.

[1] *Vide* note 5, p. 74, Illus. 6.

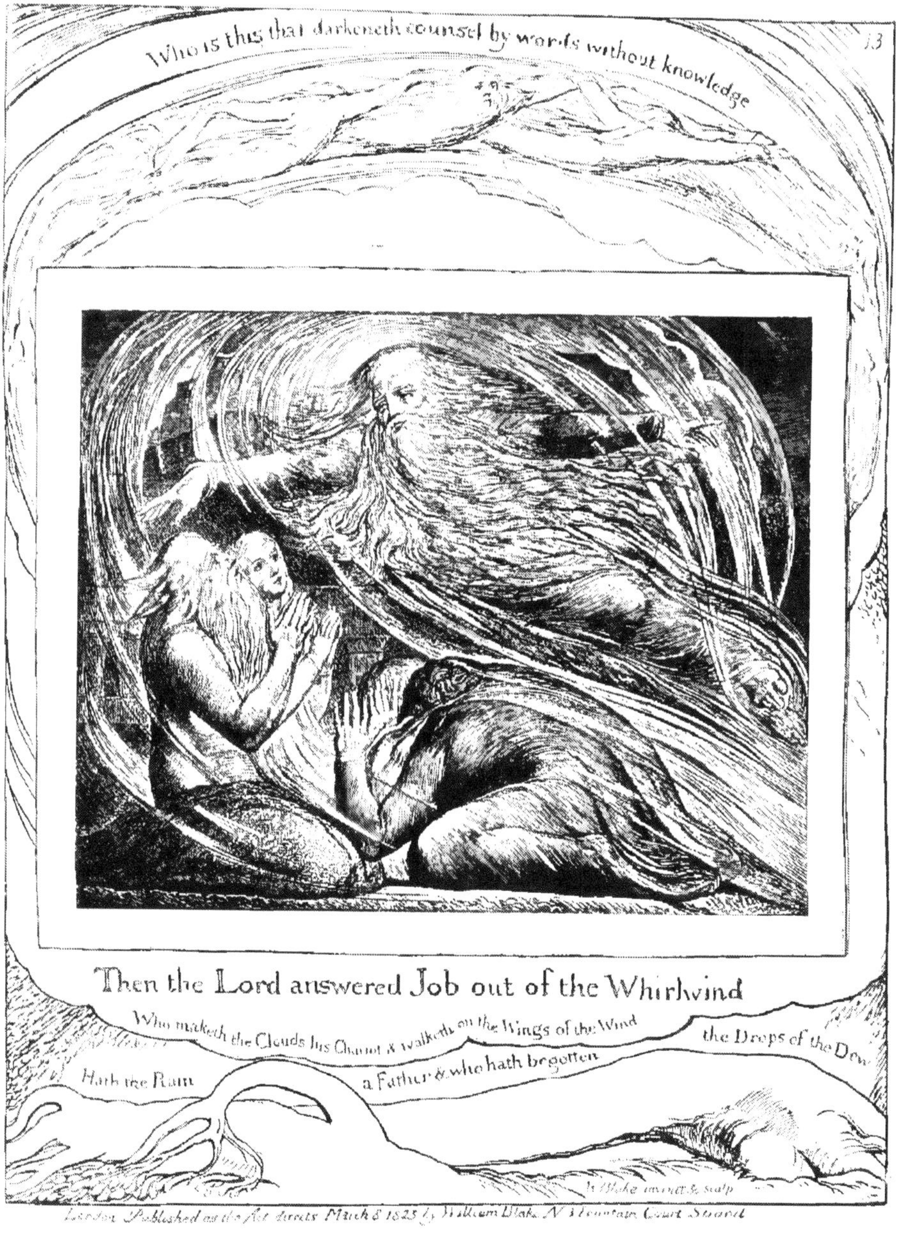
13
Who is this that darkeneth counsel by words without knowledge
Then the Lord answered Job out of the Whirlwind
Who maketh the Clouds his Chariot & walketh on the Wings of the Wind
Hath the Rain a Father & who hath begotten the Drops of the Dew
W Blake invenit & sculp
London Published as the Act directs March 8 1825 by William Blake N 3 Fountain Court Strand

ILLUSTRATION XIII

" As the seed waits eagerly watching for its flower and fruit,
Anxious its little soul looks out into the clear expanse
To see if hungry winds are abroad with their invisible array.
So Man looks out in tree, and herb, and fish, and bird, and beast,
Collecting up the scattered portions of his immortal body
Into the elemental forms of everything that grows.
He tries the sullen north wind, riding on its angry furrows,
The sultry south when the sun rises, and the angry east
When the sun sets and the clods harden and the cattle stand
Drooping, and the birds hide in their silent nests.   He stores his thoughts
As in a storehouse in his memory.   He regulates the forms
Of all beneath and all above, and in the gentle west
Reposes where the sun's heat dwells.   He rises to the sun
And to the planets of the night, and to the stars that gild
The Zodiacs, and the stars that sullen stand to north and south
He touches the remotest pole, and in the centre weeps
That Man should labour and sorrow, and learn and forget and return
To the dark valley whence he came, and begin his labour anew.
In pain he sighs, in pain he labours, and his universe
Sorrowing in birds over the deep, or howling in the wolf
Over the slain, and moaning in the cattle, and in the winds,
And weeping over Orc and Urizen in clouds and dismal fires,
And in the cries of birth and in the groans of death his voice
Is heard throughout the universe.   Wherever a grass grows
Or a leaf buds, the Eternal Man is seen, is heard, is felt,
And all his sorrows, till he re-assumes his ancient bliss."—" F. Z "

Job's new insight enables him to see his own individuality as
the clue to an immeasurably wider whole, and not the end itself.
His own capacity for pain and pleasure has taught him to feel the
joy and sorrow of the universe. Then suddenly the whirlwind
becomes vocal, and he sees in Nature's endless round, the vision of
his own Divine-humanity exalted and transfigured.[1]

[1] " F. Z.," *cp.* " Vala," viii. ll. 551-576.

The motion of the whirlwind is the same as that of the angels on the title-page, as we see by the locks of Job's hair which it lifts as it rises. The picture is the counterpart of the vision of horror in Illus. 11. The Deity moves with an upward motion in contrast to the downward motion of the former design; his outspread hands seem to bless and uplift rather than to depress and torment; and his human right foot contrasts with the sinister hoof of the evil Deity. There the serpent shows us Nature as the alien and tyrannic power whose coils we cannot escape, but here the whirlwind, while sweeping us inevitably into its round, reveals the infinite indwelling spirit which begets us, and which, in inspired moments, we recognise as our own.[1] That this is the revelation of the Divine in the Natural world, and not in the imaginative or spiritual one, is shown by the fact that Jehovah appears *beneath* the belt of clouds (dimly visible through the whirlwind) which we have already seen separating the inner and outer worlds in Illus. 2 and 5, and which we shall find used with intention "most discriminate & particular" in the next five designs.

Job's friends are at last silenced by the majesty of his vision, and his wife, on whose brow the traces of grief remain, is yet able to share with her husband the rapture of insight. If she cannot receive the truth as it was told in wrath to Job, she can appreciate it as seen by him in the perennial happenings of a

---

[1] "God is within, & without ! he is even in the depths of Hell!"
("J^m.", p. 12, l. 15.)

"Pity must join together those whom wrath has torn in sunder.
And the Religion of Generation which was meant for the destruction
Of Jerusalem, become her covering, till the time of the End.
O holy Generation, Image of regeneration !" ("J^m.", p. 7, ll. 62-65.)

". . . in Eternal Circle . . . to bring Albion again . . . into light eternal."
("J^m.", p. 75, ll. 24-26.)

ILLUSTRATION XIII   99

living creation. Job himself here appears "clothed with the Divine mercy," as the swathings of the whirlwind sweep over him.[1]

The margin carries on the motion of the whirlwind, the time current of creation, and shows Job's vision of his own spirit swept along in the endless round of Nature, "spiritually discerned." Below are the mighty roots of Nature ever strong to beget cloud, rain and wind, and even man and beast.[2]

---

[1] Though less obviously naked than in the previous designs, there is no line where the garments end on his arms or neck ; he is still "naked of natural things," till Illus. 18.

"Naked we came here—naked of natural things—and naked we shall return ; but while clothed with the Divine mercy, we are richly clothed in spiritual, and suffer all the rest gladly." Letter to Thomas Butts, 10th Jan. 1802 (Russell, pp. 101-2).

[2] The appearance of Deity in the Whirlwind below the clouds in this design is one of the most interesting points in the series, as it seems to sanction the idea of there being a divinity in outward or earthly Nature such as Blake sometimes explicitly denies, and never, perhaps, explicitly asserts, though he seems to imply it oftener than is generally admitted (e.g. "M. H. H.," p. 12, "my senses discover'd the infinite in every thing," also "J^m.", p. 12, l. 15, etc.). I cannot think that it is here a mere concession to the point of view of the Bible narrative. It is to be noted that Jehovah, though incomparably more noble than in former designs, is still in the likeness of Job, which he ceases to be in, and after, the Last Judgment (Illus. 16). And this leads me to think that Blake deliberately intends to show that outward Nature becomes real, when seen with true subjective vision. To rightly know the "subject" within, is, in fact, to find unity with the subjects outside us (men, beasts, trees, even stones, etc.), and so to be taken beyond ourselves into a greater whole, merely by going far enough into ourselves. And I suggest that this greater whole may, after all, be not so very different from the external universe as commonly conceived by the unsophisticated (vide Appendix E). At all events the "Vegetable Man" keeps something of the eternal vision lost by the reasoner (vide note 5, p. 95, etc.).

A remarkable passage in the "Milton," while showing the extent of Blake's subjectivism, clearly shows, I think, that there actually was an "outside" for him, just as real in its own way. It describes how we may start from our own minutest parts or motions ("a red Globule of Man's Blood" or "a Pulsation of the Artery"), and go inwards or outwards to immensity, though the outer is always secondary to the

inner :—   " Every Time less than a pulsation of the artery
  Is equal in its period & value to Six Thousand Years.
  [*I.e.*, roundly speaking, the whole period of history, past and future, as
    calculated, of course, upon Scriptural data.]
  For in this Period the Poets Work is Done ; and all the Great
  Events of Time start forth & are concievd in such a Period
  Within a Moment: a Pulsation of the Artery . . .

   . . . . . .

  . . . every Space larger than a red Globule of Mans blood
  Is visionary : and is created by the Hammer of Los.
  [*I.e.*, it actually exists but is the creation of the *inward.*]
  And every Space smaller than a Globule of Mans blood, opens
  Into Eternity of which this vegetable Earth is but a shadow : "
           ("Mⁿ.", p. 27, l. 62—p. 28, l. 22.)

  Sandwiched between these two passages is a somewhat whimsical, but very fine,
description of the real subjective world each of us lives in.

  " The Sky is an immortal Tent built by the Sons of Los
  And every Space that a Man views around his dwelling-place,
  Standing on his own roof, or in his garden on a mount
  Of twentyfive cubits in height, such space is his Universe :
  And on its verge the Sun rises & sets, the Clouds bow
  To meet the flat Earth & the Sea in such an orderd Space .
  The Starry heavens reach no further but here bend and set
  On all sides, & the two Poles turn on their valves of gold :
  And if he move his dwelling-place, his heavens also move.
  Wher'eer he goes & all his neighbourhood bewail his loss :
  Such are the Spaces called Earth & such its dimension :
  As to that false appearance which appears to the reasoner,
  As of a Globe rolling thro Voidness, it is a delusion of Ulro
  The Microscope knows not of this nor the Telescope, they alter
  The ratio of the Spectators Organs but leave Objects untouchd."
           ("Mⁿ.", p. 28, ll. 4-18.)

  Yet notwithstanding this intense subjectivism, Blake constantly admits that Eternity
is to be found " without " as well as " within " (" J^m.", p. 12, l. 15, etc.), and I can
but suppose that he finds it in the life of other beings and loses it only in the non-
human environment which appears to separate those lives.

  " The Vegetative Universe opens like a flower from the Earths center
  In which is Eternity.   It expands in Stars to the Mundane Shell
  And there it meets Eternity again, both within and without,
  And the abstract voids between the Stars are the Satanic Wheels."
           " J^m.", p. 13, ll. 34-37

(for the significance of the Satanic Wheels *vide* Appendix D).

14

Canst thou bind the sweet influences of Pleiades or loose the bands of Orion

Let there Be
Light

Let there be a
Firmament

Let the Waters be
gathered into one place

& let the Dry Land
appear

And God made Two Great Lights

Let the Waters bring
forth abundantly

Let the Earth bring forth

Cattle & Creeping thing
& Beast

When the morning Stars sang together, & all the
Sons of God shouted for joy

London. Published as the Act directs March 8. 1825 by Will. Blake N3 Fountain Court Strand.

ILLUSTRATION XIV

". . . all Animals & Vegetations, the Earth & Heaven, were containd in the All Glorious Imagination" ("Jm.", p. 49, ll. 13-14).

"The Imagination is not a State : it is the Human Existence itself" ("Mn", p. 32*, l. 32).

In this great design, where Blake touches the height of his genius, and, indeed, of genius itself, he shows the perennial act of spiritual Creation ever going on in the "Bosom of God, the Human Imagination," and the fusion of this with Universal reality beyond.

The rolling layers of cloud divide the design into the four great worlds of vision, united by the Divine Being who appears, as before, in the spiritual likeness of Job, with right foot uncovered in contrast to the uncovered left foot of the earthly man. Below is the world of time and space ; the world as it appears to our bodily senses, shut off from everything but the earth. Above this opens the eternal world within. Here dwells the spiritual Creator, the light of life that illumines the whole universe, but can only be known in its true subjective reality in the here and the now and the me. This inner world is divided into two. Beneath the Deity's right arm there rides forth the sun of the mind,[1] driving the horses of instruction ;[2] while beneath his left arm the moon of poetic, or woman's love,[3] controls and guides the serpents of

[1] "F. Z." ("Vala," i. ll. 287-9) cp. "Jm.", p. 24, l 10.
[2] "M. H. H.," p. 9; "F. Z." ("Vala," ii l. 35)
[3] Cp. ". . . Beulahs moony shades and hills
    Within the Human Heart." ("Jm.", p. 48, ll. 24-5),
with "Beulah, a soft, moony universe, feminine, lovely" ("F. Z.," cp. "Vala," i. l. 204). (In the Book of Isaiah, lxii. 4, the land of Israel is to be called "Beulah" בעולה [to signify that it is no more desolate, but is "married," from בעל to possess, to take to wife.)

corporeal desires.[1]   Love and thought are perennial features of the
Divine-Humanity which Blake sometimes associates with Night[2]
and Morning[3] and here perhaps connects with the words of the
Bible " the evening and the morning were the first day . . . and
the evening and the morning were the sixth day."

Between these and the seraphs above, we have a glimpse into
the empty abyss representing the void of Nature—the unknown,
where we cannot trace the presence of the Divine-humanity.   But
beyond this again is the universe of stars—the infinite life beyond
our life, multitudinous in sea and air and the countless generations
of men, with which our Eternal Being, bridging the gulf of Nature,
links us in sympathy and spiritual unity.   The seraphs are the Sons
of God, the poetic emanations of the Divine-Human Imagination.[4]
These mingling with the Morning Stars adjoin " Man to Man " and
waken harmonies of so intense a joy, that it seems to tremble on
the verge of a great sob, in which the eternal grief of the universe
is merged in its eternal rapture.   " Excess of joy is like excess
of grief." [5]

---

[1] *Cp.* " J^m.", p. 55, ll. 11-13, etc.
[2] *Cp. supra* note 3, p. 101, and also last two verses of " William Bond."

> I thought Love lived in the hot sunshine,
> But O, he lives in the Moony light !
> I thought to find Love in the heat of Day,
> But sweet Love is the Comforter of Night.
>
> Seek Love in the Pity of others' Woe
> In the gentle relief of another's care,
> In the darkness of night & the Winters' Snow,
> In the naked & outcast, seek Love there !   (Sampson, p. 298.)

[3] *Cp. supra* note 1, p. 101, for association of Urizen with the brain and " F. Z."
(" Vala," ix. l. 647) for his association with Morning.
[4] *Cp.* Illus. 12.
[5] " F. Z.," *cp.* " Vala," ix. l. 727 ; *cp.* also " M. H. H.," p. 8.

ILLUSTRATION XIV   103

The uplifted arms of the seraphs, like the outspread ones of the Deity below, are probably symbolic of the active life, which brings us into relations with our fellow-beings, giving meaning and liberty to our inward lives, and breaking down the barriers with which the merely speculative intellect bounds itself.[1] Blake's inspired after-thought ‘ which led him to add the arms and wings seen appearing from beyond the margin on either side, reinforces the idea of the illimitable character, and united strength of, man's mental life, when it has found its relations to the universal life.[3]

Although the passion and splendour of this design do not depend for their appeal upon our knowing its meaning—for it is, indeed, almost equally great as an illustration of Genesis or Job or Blakean Christianity—it is easy to see why the conception of Love, rising from within but becoming active and multitudinous in relation to its objects, could move Blake to so great a height of joy. Wordsworth, it will be remembered, speaking of the " transcendent peace " which waited on his mathematical studies, says : " mighty is the charm of those abstractions to a mind beset with images and haunted by herself." And Blake's mind imprisoned by temperament and conviction in its own seething inner world, found its escape, not in the timeless abstractions which for Wordsworth in his youth typified " the one Supreme Existence," but in the practical reality of other souls ; of human

[1] *Vide* Illus. 9 and 10.

[2] *Vide* Gilchrist, ii p. 224.

[3] There are two illustrations in " Jerusalem " completely different in design but probably closely similar in conception ; both as compared with the present illustration, and with each other. In each case linked angels form a chain across the design, and in one case the text proves that they symbolise the interlinking thoughts of Love, that unite man with his universe, and give it a spiritual unity, as opposed to the lower unities of materialism, shown below. (" J^{m}.", pp. 22 and 75, *vide* Appendix D.)

"particulars," as he himself would have called them.   The discovery of the Supreme Existence in our fellow-beings, interpreted by our own being, kindled "peace," for Blake, into rapture.

In a later design we shall see how the final crisis of Job's life is reached when the vision of this truth wins the passionate allegiance of his active Will.

The little angels at the upper corners in the margin are unrolling the thread of truth that leads us out of the labyrinth of this life.

> "I give you the end of a golden string,
>   Only wind it into a ball :
>   It will lead you in at Heavens gate,
>   Built in Jerusalems wall." [1]

The margin below shows the flames and foaming abyss of Time and Space [2] in which the worm and the dread serpent roll—cut off by clouds from the spheres that enclose the days of poetic creation, but with access to the region of stars (note the rising flame on the spectator's right reaching up to the fourth day) ; for the stars are common to both worlds.

[1] "Jm.", p. 77, ll. 1-4.
[2] "Behind, the sea of time and space roars and follows swiftly.   He who keeps not right onwards is lost."   Letter to Thomas Butts, 10th Jan. 1802 (Russell, p. 100).

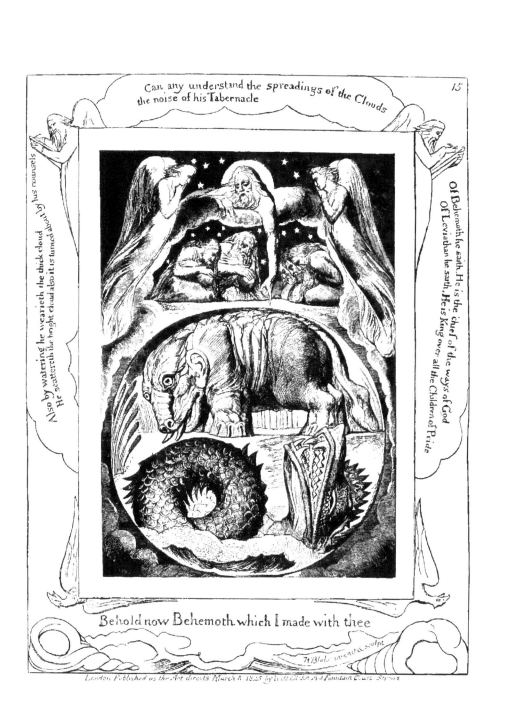

15

Can any understand the spreadings of the Clouds
the noise of his Tabernacle

Also by watering he wearieth the thick cloud
He scattereth the bright cloud also it is turned about by his counsels

Of Behemoth he saith. He is the chief of the ways of God
Of Leviathan he saith. He is King over all the Children of Pride

Behold now Behemoth which I made with thee

WBlake invent & sculpt

London Published as the Act directs March 8 1825 by Will Blake N 3 Fountain Court Strand

ILLUSTRATION XV

" Rolling the Sea in rocky paths ; forming Leviathan
And Behemoth ; the War by Sea enormous & the War
By Land astounding : erecting pillars in the deepest Hell,
To reach the heavenly arches : " (" J^m.", p. 91, ll. 38-41.) [1]

THIS design shows us the creation of the outer or natural world, which to Blake seemed but a shadow of the world within.[2] In the foregoing the Deity points with right forefinger towards the stars, while the mortal men below gaze up in rapture. Now he points with left hand down to the regions below man, though included in the mundane belt of clouds. Here are the monstrous forms of the sea- and earth-powers with their animal and vegetable life, terrible in their magnitude and their might, but unillumined by intelligence, or the knowledge of " brotherhood." Yet these are the works of the same life-power as we know in ourselves though as yet but half revealed.

[1] This is the work of Los's Spectre. Los is lord of Time and Space (" Time & Space obey my will," " M^n.", p. 20, l. 17), and works with his Spectre for the redemption of Humanity (" J^m.", p 8, ll. 39, 40). The Spectre is often defined as the Reasoning power, but really represents the " Natural man" in every aspect (" Man is born a Spectre or Satan," " J^m.", p. 52 ; *cp*. " The Devil is in us, as far as we are Nature." " H. C. R. Diary," 24th Dec. 1825 ; Symons, p. 265).

The work of Los's Spectre, then, is of the natural creation in Time and Space (*cp* last four lines of long passage quoted from the " Milton " in note to Illus. 13, and note the *reasoner's* vision of the universe) which is created to be destroyed and so separated or cast out (*cp*. note 4, p. 21, Preface). In the passage from which the above lines are quoted, Los destroys the works of the Spectre, until at last he has " completely divided him into a separate space," " J^m ", p. 91, l. 52 (*cp*. " Giving a body to Falshood that it may be cast off for ever," " J^m.", p. 12, l. 13).

[2] " In your Imagination of which this World of Mortality is but a Shadow " (" J^m.", p. 71, l. 19).

The elemental stars appear in the natural world as well as in the eternal world above the clouds; for they are the link between nature and eternity.[1]

The margin shows again the abysmal deep, and the spiral shells that express in another form the coil of revolving and evolving life. The corners are set with symbols of light and air, the two elements needed to supplement earth and water, and of which the spiritual aspects—love and knowledge[2]—are yet wanting to the perfect creation.

---

[1] "F. Z ," "Vala," ii. ll. 266, 267. *Vide* Illus. 12.

[2] We may find the correspondence of the Zoas with the elements in "F. Z." ("Vala," i. ll. 285-290). Here Los describes the other three Zoas: "Luvah walking upon the winds!" "the Human Brain, where Urizen and all his hosts hang their immortal lamps;" and "this cold expanse where watery Tharmas mourns." Here we have also evidence of the relation of Urizen (light) with the human mind. And Luvah says, "I was Love," in "F. Z " ("Vala," ii. l. 104). Thus we get Light corresponding to mind and Air to love, and we may therefore take the eagles to represent love, the old man intellect, and the two to supplement Leviathan and Behemoth as the water and earth powers.

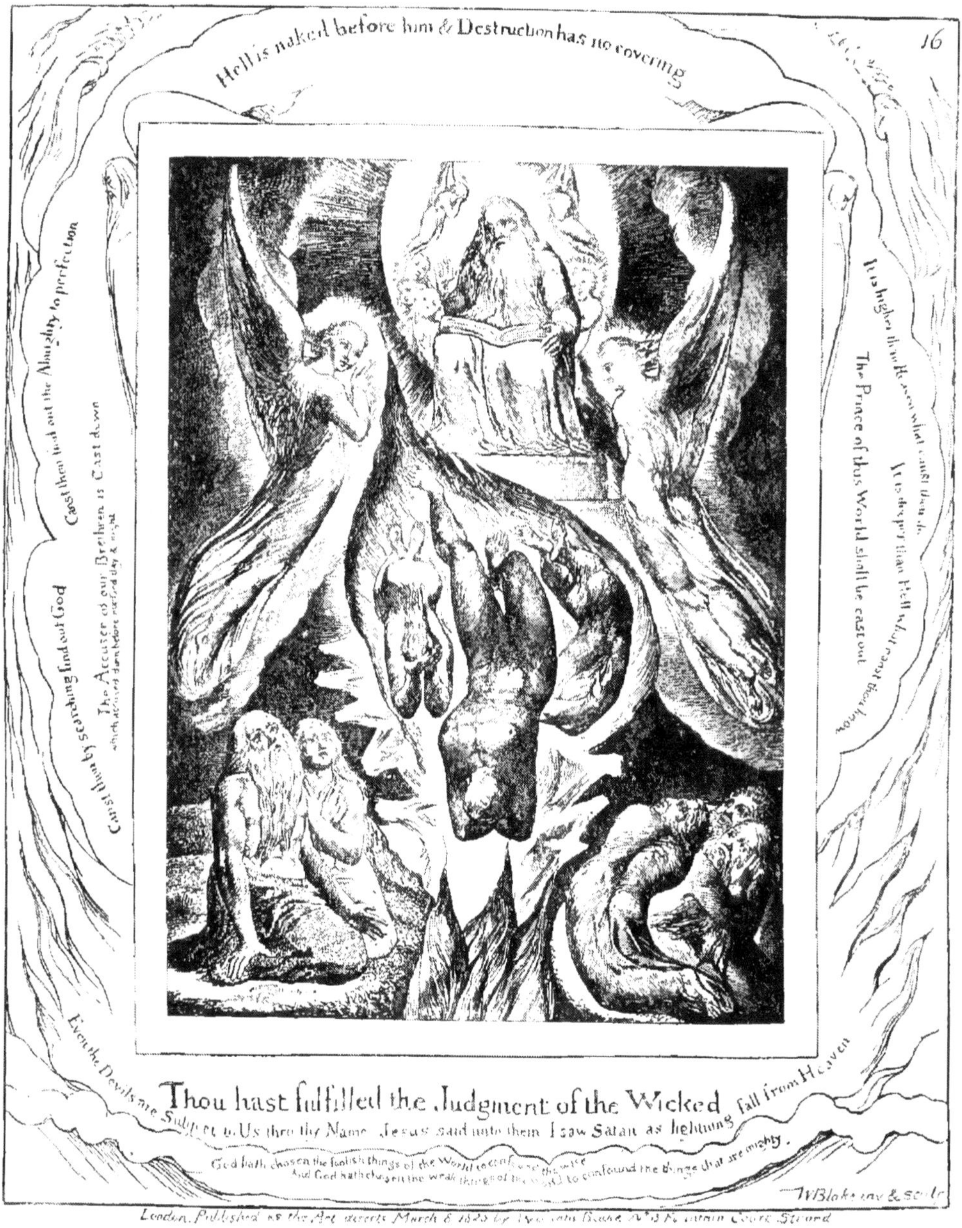
16
Hell is naked before him & Destruction has no covering
Canst thou by searching find out God
Canst thou find out the Almighty to perfection
The Accuser of our Brethren is Cast down
It is higher than Heaven what canst thou do
It is deeper than Hell what canst thou know
The Prince of this World shall be cast out
Thou hast fulfilled the Judgment of the Wicked
Even the Devils are Subject to Us thro thy Name. Jesus said unto them I saw Satan as lightning fall from Heaven
God hath chosen the foolish things of the World to confound the wise
And God hath chosen the weak things of the World to confound the things that are mighty
W Blake inv & sculp
London, Published as the Act directs March 8 1825 by William Blake No 3 Fountain Court Strand

ILLUSTRATION XVI

" Forgiveness of sin is only at the judgment-seat of Jesus the Saviour, where the accuser
is cast out." "V. L J" (Gilchrist, ii. p. 199).

THIS design (like Illus. 6 in the descent) is typical of the whole
process of ascent rather than of any single episode. Four out of
the eight texts are from the New Testament and the other four
are all from the earlier parts of the book of Job. It represents
what Blake calls a "Last Judgment," or the casting out of error.
"Whenever any individual rejects error, and embraces truth,"
Blake says, "a Last Judgment passes upon that individual."[1] By
means of this, Job and his wife are to be lifted to a yet more
perfect vision.

In the second Illustration we saw the evil Job and wife
appearing as shadowy images in Satan's flame. Now we see in
Satan's flame these evil selves as they have been bodied forth into
a permanent form, making it possible to cast them out for ever
with the great Satan himself.[2] Job will never again be tempted
to mistake his own personal salvation or even his own righteousness for life's true end. And meanwhile his own sufferings have
wakened his imaginative life, and begotten in him a tender sympathy for the spiritual labour and sorrow of all creation. For

---

[1] Gilchrist, ii. p. 196.
[2] " To be an error, and to be cast out, is a part of God's design." "V. L. J."
(Gilchrist, ii. p. 195)
  Cp. " F. Z." (" Vala," viii. p. 475.) " All mortal things made permanent that
they may be put off."

into the light of the divine sun or halo, there enter the many forms of children, representing "the eternal births of intellect from the divine humanity" [1] while the little weeping angels [2] speak of the Pity by which the wars of the world produced by Wrath can alone be healed. [3]

Job's friends narrowly escape the blast that sweeps down the evil ones to destruction. [4] There is something in their souls over which it has power, but they are saved, as we shall see, by the compassion of Job's Divine-humanity. For, fortunately, we have not all to go down to the pit's depth, if we can learn from the experience of others. [5]

It should be noticed that the belt of clouds which has always separated earth from heaven is at last broken through, making a clear passage from one to the other.

---

[1] "Jesus is surrounded by beams of glory, in which are seen all around Him infants emanating from Him . these represent the eternal births of intellect from the divine humanity." "V. L. J." (Gilchrist, ii. p. 196).

[2] "Every Tear from Every Eye
Becomes a Babe in Eternity:"
"Auguries of Innocence," ll 67-68 (Sampson, p. 290).

[3] "They have divided themselves by Wrath, they must be united by Pity" ("Jm.", p. 7, ll. 57-8).

[4] "Hope earnestly that you have escaped the brush of my evil star, which I believe is now for ever fallen into the abyss." Letter to Hayley, 27th Jan. 1804 (Russell, p. 141).

[5] Vide p. 123, Illus. 18.

17

He bringeth down to the Grave & bringeth up

We know that when he shall appear we shall be like him for we shall see him as He Is

When I behold the Heavens the work of thy hands the Moon & Stars which thou hast ordained then I say What is Man that thou art mindful of him & the Son of Man that thou visitest him

I have heard thee with the hearing of the Ear but now my Eye seeth thee

He that hath seen me

hath seen my Father also
I & my Father are One

If ye had known me ye would have known my Father also

Believe me that I am in the Father & the Father in me

At that day ye shall know that I am in
my Father & you in me & I in you
If ye loved me ye would rejoice
because I said I go unto the Father

London Published as the Act directs March 8 1825 by William Blake N 3 Fountain Court Strand

ILLUSTRATION XVII

"He who would see the Divinity must see him in his Children
One first, in friendship & love: then a Divine Family, & in the midst
Jesus will appear." ("Jm.", p. 91, ll. 18-20.)

THE same act of Judgment which materialises the Satanic element
of existence that it may be "cast off for ever," also defines the
Christ element. "Heaven & Hell are born together,"[1] and the
great rupture that sends the corporealised Satan into the Abyss
sends the Christ in bodily form to earth. "The Last Judgment,"
Blake says, "is seen by the eye of every one according to the
situation he holds."[2] And what appears from one point of
view as the descent of Satan will be from another the ascent of
Christ.[3] The present Illustration therefore represents the lines in
" Jerusalem " :—

"But Jesus breaking thro' the Central Zones of Death & Hell
Opens Eternity in Time & Space : triumphant in Mercy."[4]

In the margin below, Jerusalem, bride of the Lamb,[5] unfolds
the scriptures-descriptive of the Incarnate Word, in whom Job and
his wife at last see God as he is ; no longer in the likeness of
Job alone, but as the soul of the whole race and the universe—the
universal Divine-Humanity itself.

"As One Man all the Universal Family : and that One Man
We call Jesus the Christ : and he in us, and we in him,
Live in perfect harmony in Eden the land of life,
Giving, receiving, and forgiving each others trespasses."[6]

---

[1] "Swed.," p. 458 (Blake's last note).
[2] Last sentence of the " Vision of the Last Judgment." (Gilchrist, II. 200.)
[3] Cp. " M. H. H.," pp. 5 and 6. " It indeed appear'd to Reason as if Desire was
cast out, but the Devils account is, that the Messiah fell, & formed a heaven of what
he stole from the Abyss."
[4] "Jm.", p. 75, ll. 21, 22.   [5] "Jm.", p. 27, etc.
[6] "Jm.", p. 38, l. 19 ff; cp. also Ibid., p. 96, ll. 3-6, etc.

To Job and his wife this human God is a presence of pure beneficence, but to Eliphaz and his friends it is a terrible figure of judgment.   For their Deity had been one from whom all that was lovely or human was sternly excluded,[1] so that when they see the perfect manhood manifested in all its convincing glory, they turn away in humiliation and terror.

Here again the belt of clouds is used with great significance, showing the difference between this revelation of Deity, and that in the whirlwind.   There the Divine-life appeared *below* the clouds in the natural world.   It represented " God des[c]ending according to the weakness of man."[2]   Here on the other hand the earthly men are themselves lifted *above* the clouds by the light of God, who puts the Abyss for ever beneath them (note the empty space in the lower corner of the design, behind Christ, on the spectator's left).   Job's earlier visions of God before the " Last Judgment " were of God in Nature, and in all those Jehovah still appeared in the likeness of Job ; perhaps because it is only by analogy with his own consciousness that a man can read the Divine life in the worm and the clod.   But after a Last Judgment, when he has finally realised and thrown away the natural self-seeking man, he acquires "a New Selfhood continually"[3] living, even while still in body, only in, and for, the Universal Humanity, symbolised by Christ.   God descends into creation that man may be enabled to ascend therefrom.   " He is become a worm, that he may nourish the weak,"[4] or, as Blake quotes in his little engraved pamphlet, " Therefore God becomes as we are, that we may be as he is."[5]   The whirlwind design represented God becoming Man, this design represents

[1] *Vide* Illus. 9.   [2] " Lav.", 630 (*cp.* Ellis, 620, p. 149).
[3] " J^m.", p. 52.   [4] " Lav.", 630 (*cp.* Ellis, 620, p. 149).
[5] " N.N. R. (a)," (E. & Y., in.).

ILLUSTRATION XVII   111

Man becoming God. But, to at all understand Blake's conception
of Man becoming God, and the place of Christ in his pantheism, it
is necessary to have some knowledge of his idea of the "Divine-
Humanity,"—and though this is not very simple it will, more than
anything else, explain his final message in these last designs.

(Some readers may prefer to omit this section till the remaining designs have been examined.)

Of Jesus he said, "*He is the only God,*" but added, "and so am
I and so are you."[1] And although the general purport of this
characteristic saying is clear enough, its lucidity and significance
will be greatly increased by a knowledge of his distinction between
"Identity" and "Essence"; a distinction which it is worth while
to be at the pains to understand.

Each man has his own distinct and eternal Identity, which is not
the same as any other, and can never be altered or destroyed or lost
in something else. "Individual Identities never change nor cease."[2]

But while constantly insisting on the permanence of "identities,"
Blake believes that all men (and things) are One in "essence," or,
as we might say, in their ultimate nature or character. "One and
the same Identity," says Swedenborg, "is not communicable,"
"but one & the same Essence is,"[3] adds Blake.

Now it is this essence, or ultimate human character, which he
calls God, or the true Man,[4] and it is possible to view the Universe
either as the one Essence (God) or as many Identities (men and
things).

"... contracting our infinite senses
We behold multitude: or expanding; we behold as one."[5]

[1] "H. C. R. Diary," 10th Dec. 1825 (Symons, p. 255). Italics H. C. R.'s.
[2] "Mⁿ.", p. 32*, l. 23 (Extra page).
[3] "Swed.," p. 24.
[4] "N. N. R. (b)," (E. & Y., iii.).
[5] "Jm.", p. 38, ll. 17-18.

When we look at it as essence it is God and nothing else. "Creation is God des[c]ending according to the weakness of man, for our Lord is the word of God, & everything on earth is the word of God, & in its essence is God."[1] But when on the other hand we are thinking of identities, God is to be conceived as existing only in these. "God only Acts & Is, in existing beings or Men."[2] "The worship of God is, Honouring his gifts in other men . . . for there is no other God."[3] "The Infinite alone resides in Definite & Determinate Identity."[4] Yet the relation of the identities and their essence is clear enough, and is the same as that between various thoughts and a single emotion from which they spring. "From Essence proceeds Identity, & from one Essence may proceed many Identities, as from one Affection may proceed many thoughts."[5] So every man and thing is due to the same vital essence, as many thoughts may be due to one affection. To complete the parallel we have only to add, what Blake perhaps intended to imply, that the affection must be present in *some* thought to exist at all—for, as we have seen, he constantly says that God, the unity, has no existence except in some man ; Jesus, or you, or me.

That this is in substance the outline of Blake's theological system, there can be little or no doubt. Though principally gathered from earlier philosophic writings, it entirely accords with

---

[1] "Lav.", p. 630 (*cp.* Ellis, 620, p. 149).

[2] "M. H. H.," p. 16.

[3] *Ibid.* p. 22*f*; *cp.* "J^m.", p. 91, ll. 7-10.

[4] "J^m.", p. 55, l. 64. *Cp.* "But General Forms have their vitality in Particulars : & every Particular is a Man : " ("J^m.", p. 91, ll. 29-30.)

[5] "Swed.," p. 24. The remark, "From Essence proceeds Identity," means, of course, more than that men are made by God. It means that the quality of *Identity* in a man—that which makes him *himself* and no one else—*is* his essence, God.

ILLUSTRATION XVII 113

similar expressions in his "Jerusalem," and it explains what he meant in his last years when (as Crabb Robinson says) "he denied that God has any power,"[1] and declared that the language of the Bible as to God's omnipotence was "poetical or allegorical."[2]

But if the Essence, God, does not exist as a separate personality, apart from human identities, what does Blake mean when he talks of the "Father"; of "the Eternal Mercy"; of the ordering of the "Divine Hand"; and so forth?

In the first place, it must be remembered that he freely personifies all his thoughts, "for it is impossible to think without images of somewhat on earth."[3] In the next place, even when he uses expressions which seem to refer to the Creator, he is probably really thinking of the Eternal Christ, the typical (though with Blake, not the only) embodiment of the Divine Essence.

But even so, there are passages which seem at first difficult to reconcile with his system. In certain places he seems to speak of God as presiding over, and guiding, the evolutions of Nature, and in others of Him as sharing the suffering of His creatures. How can an essence, we ask ourselves, which only exists in individuals and has no omnipotence, or even power, be conceived as watching over, suffering in, and guiding the whole?

While freely admitting that the attempt to read philosophic consistency into a poet of bold and soaring inspirations may be easily carried too far, I cannot but think that in this particular case it is amply justified by the result.

In the first place, outward nature, though it is for Blake essentially "the work of the Devil,"[4] has never been in any part

[1] "H. C. R. Diary," 24th Dec. 1825 (Symons, p. 265).
[2] *Ibid.*, 17th Dec. 1825 (Symons, p. 263).
[3] "Lav." (final note), (Ellis, p. 151).
[4] "H. C. R. Diary," 24th Dec. 1825 (Symons, p. 265).

H

wholly without the active spirit of love, and life, working as a blind and sleeping force, perhaps, but nevertheless working, and always towards the light. However overlaid and defaced, the true "essence" is always *there*, wherever existence comes. "God is within & without; he is even in the depths of Hell." [1] And it is possible to read the following remarkable passage from the "Four Zoas" in this way; as a description of how the vital essence is never wholly obliterated from the evolutions of nature.

> "The ever pitying one who seeth all things, saw his fall,
> And in the dark vacuity created a bosom of clay.
> When wearied, dead, he fell, his limbs repos'd in the bosom of slime.
> As the seed falls from the sower's hand, so Urizen fell; and death
> Shut up his powers in oblivion: then as the seed shoots forth
> In pain & sorrow, So the slimy bed his limbs renew'd.
> At first an infant weakness: periods pass'd, he gather'd strength,
>
> Endless had been his travel, but the Divine hand him led.
> For infinite the distance & obscur'd by Combustions dire,
> By rocky masses frowning in the abysses revolving erratic,
> Round Lakes of fire in the dark deep." [2]

A very beautiful, but for the interpreter still more difficult passage is one from " Jerusalem ":—

> "For not one sparrow can suffer, & the whole Universe not suffer also,
> In all its Regions, & its Father & Saviour not pity and weep." [3]

This passage, I do not doubt, represents a genuine and perhaps frequent aspect of Blake's spiritual vision. It is the Universe seen in the eternal "identity" of Christ. But as such it is certainly not peculiar to Blake, nor even, I think, especially characteristic. Blake certainly does not think that we are each fragments of a universal body, analogous to the earthly body, and of which Christ

[1] "Jm.", p. 12, l. 15.   [2] "F. Z." ("Vala," vi. ll. 154-176).
[3] Jm.", p. 25, ll. 8, 9.

ILLUSTRATION XVII   115

is the soul, as this passage seems to imply.[1] And before we can understand it in its richer sense, we must re-translate this vision into the vision of multitude—or as he would call it, the contracted vision—and so lead ourselves up to his true " expanded " vision of a unity of essence.

To do this, we must remember that it is in virtue of his *love*[2] that the " Saviour " becomes the Whole and feels for, and in, the whole. Now love is *our* essence as well as Christ's,[3] and for this reason " you " and " I " may also become the Whole in so far as we attain perfect love. " For if a thing loves it is infinite." [4] This is to become ourselves the essential unity, and the Universe " in all its parts " is the whole knit into unity by the spirit of love, the Father, in "you" and " me."

Now it is this fact that each of us may live the universal life, which is the great thing we have in common with all others. This constitutes our unity of essence, and is the only unity that exists, as it is the only unity that matters. This leads us to the last and most vital point in the system.

In so far as the love dwelling in any of us achieves this unifying of all life, it does so *not* by merging all identities in our own, but

---

[1] For Christ (or God) to be the dominant " identity," uniting the whole into a single consciousness, would be anathema to Blake. " If all but God is not Infinite they shall come to an End which God forbid. If the Essence was the same as the Identity there could be but one Identity, which is false. Heaven would upon this plan be but a Clock " (" Swed.," p. 24). That is to say, a mechanism of wheels, only unified by external contact and driving each other by compulsion (*vide* Appendix D. on " The Satanic Wheels "), each part a mere mechanical fragment of a single and identical Whole. Or perhaps one of a mere series of single moments, instead of an eternal interpenetrating Present, in which every moment is equally eternal and all-comprehensive. *Cp.* " Jm.", p. 15, l. 8, and " F. Z." (" Vala," ix. 170), and " Lav." (*vide supra*, p. 10, note 1).

[2] " Jm.", p. 43, ll. 19-23 (*vide* next page).   [3] *Ibid.*, p. 96, ll. 26, 27.

[4] " Swed.," p. 40.

by recognising and reverencing the eternal identities of others. We must realise that "In *every* bosom a Universe expands."[1] For indeed "How do you know but ev'ry Bird that cuts the airy way, Is an immense world of delight, clos'd by your senses five?"[2]

Love (or benevolence as Blake calls it in the passage below, for he is constantly at pains to distinguish the love of self-surrender from the love of self-seeking),[3] imaginative love, the love of friendship and brotherhood, is the unifying essence, just because it alone reverences the sanctity of individual identities.[4] In a passage in the "Jerusalem," the "Divine-Humanity," which he describes as the "Only General and Universal Form," is identified with "benevolence, *Who protects minute particulars, every one in their own identity.*"[5]

Before passing to the next design, one further illustration, though not drawn immediately from Blake himself, may help to elucidate this great conception of the relations of the Essence and Identities. Certain pinnacles of art, we all feel, have a mysterious kinship and even oneness, rendered only the more impressive by their exterior remoteness. Dante's final vision of the Divine Light, Beethoven's last Sonata,[6] Blake's Song of the Morning Stars[7]—are creations not only of different arts and different masters,

---

[1] "Jm.", p. 38, l. 49 (italics mine).   [2] "M. H H.," p. 7.
[3] *Cp.* "The Clod & the Pebble," "S. of E.," and "Jm.", p. 33, l. 52, and context. Also "Affection or Love becomes a State, when divided from Imagination" ("Mn.", p. 32,* l. 33, extra page). "Without Forgiveness of Sin Love is Itself Eternal Death" ("Jm.", p. 64, l. 24).
[4] "For the Sanctuary of Eden is . . .
In the Circumference; & every Minute Particular is Holy:"
("Jm.", p. 69, ll. 41, 42).
[5] "Jm.", p. 43, ll. 19-23 (italics mine).
[6] Opus 111.
[7] Illus. 14. A suggestive comparison between the Choral Symphony and Blake's 14th Job Illus. will be found in the Study of his art, by Irene Langridge ("William Blake," Geo. Bell & Sons, p. 155).

ILLUSTRATION XVII   117

but extraordinarily different in the ideas they treat, in mastery of technique and in methods of approach. Yet each in turn seems gifted with power to lift the mind into the same region of spiritual light, each seems the vehicle of the same supreme aspiration and fulfilment, each in short seems the utterance of the same final human genius, the same ultimately divine essence.

And though this essence only " is " when realised in some actual " vision," its mysterious presence makes the vehicle transcend the limitations of all art and become something more universal than either pictures or poetry or even music itself.

But Blake's " God " is the essence not of human visions or creations, but of human beings themselves. You cannot indeed have the essence of Man without men. But since the essence is itself love or imagination, the man becomes something immeasurably greater than himself in proportion to his realisation of himself. Every human identity, while always freely and independently active, is essentially one with all others as it becomes more perfect. This is Job's vision of Christ, which we are to see in the following designs becoming not only a Vision, but a life.[1]

[1] For the further treatment of this subject, *vide* Appendix E. on Blake's " Pluralism," pp. 141 *ff.*

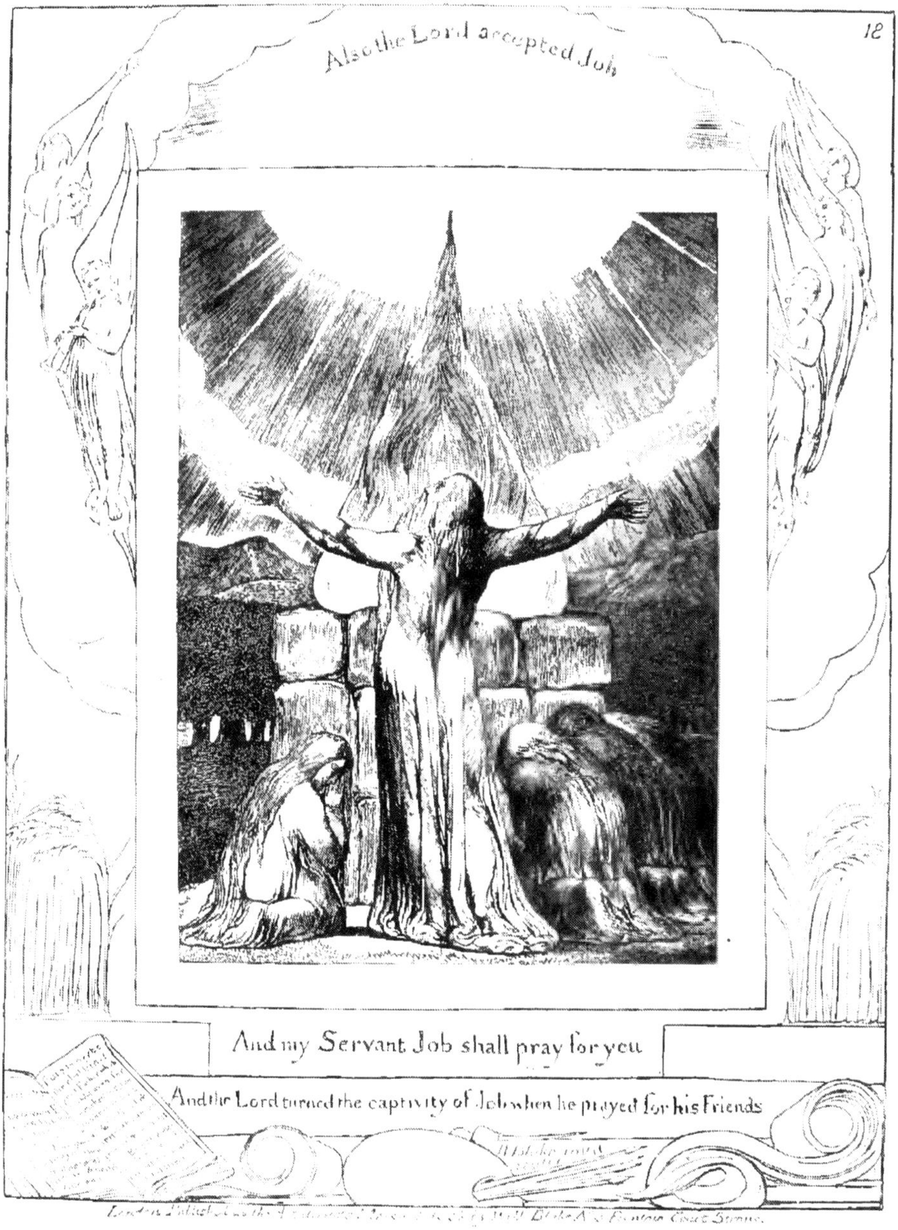
18
Also the Lord accepted Job
And my Servant Job shall pray for you
And the Lord turned the captivity of Job when he prayed for his Friends

ILLUSTRATION XVIII

"This is Jerusalem in every Man
A Tent & Tabernacle of Mutual Forgiveness . . . ." ("Jᵐ.", p. 54, ll. 3, 4)

"THE Lord also accepted Job . . . when he prayed for his friends."[1] Forgiveness, according to Blake, is the entrance to Paradise;[2] the Divine life becoming reconciled to our earthly lives in so far only as these are reconciled to one another.[3] To feel resentment or anger against a wrong-doer, is to forget that he himself is the greatest sufferer, and, therefore, the most needing our compassion.[4]

[1] Job xlii. 9, 10.
[2] Prologue to the small engraved pamphlet, "For the Sexes, The Gates of Paradise." Sampson, p. 372.
"Mutual Forgiveness of each Vice
Such are the gates of Paradise."
Cp. " The Glory of Christianity is, To Conquer by Forgiveness."
("Jᵐ.", p. 52 ; cp. Ibid., p. 64, l. 24, etc.)
[3] " . . . If you Forgive one-another so shall Jehovah Forgive You:
That He Himself may Dwell among You."
("Jᵐ.", p. 61, ll. 25, 26.)
[4] " If I should dare to lay my finger on a grain of sand
In way of vengeance : I punish the already punishd : O whom
Should I pity if I pity not the sinner who is gone astray : "
("Jᵐ.", p. 31, ll. 33-35.)
Cp. " Go therefore cast out devils in Christs name,
Heal thou the sick of spiritual disease.
Pity the evil, for thou art not sent
To smite with terror & with punishments
Those that are sick, like to the Pharisees
Crucifying & encompas(s)ing sea & land
For proselytes to tyranny & wrath,
But to the Publicans & Harlots go ;
Teach them True Happiness, but let no curse
Go forth out of thy mouth to blight their peace.
For Hell is opend to Heaven ; thine eyes beheld
The dungeons burst & the Prisoners set free." ("Jᵐ.", p. 77, poem.)

But it is hard to forgive those who have lightly condemned us. Job has been harassed in his spiritual struggle by his friends' arrogant assumption of superiority. Yet, now that he has been vindicated by the incarnate Deity (Illus. 17), he is not to indulge even a momentary sense of triumph or satisfaction at their rebuff, but is called on to freely share with them the truth he has bought so dearly and in their despite.

So far Blake does no more than treat sympathetically the episode as he found it in the Bible. But he could not fail to use the design to express his own remoter thoughts, for which we must now look. There can be no doubt that the altar and flame have a symbolical meaning, and do not literally illustrate the Bible story. For, in the first place, Blake shows us nothing of the "seven bullocks and seven rams"[1] brought by the friends for the sacrifice, and we shall notice that, in the margin of Illus. 21, the text upon the altar expressly quotes: "In burnt Offerings for Sin thou hast had no Pleasure," which may satisfy us that Blake did not intend to represent a literal burnt-offering as the occasion of Job's acceptance.

The design is again[2] divided by a belt of clouds into the world above and the world below, or, rather, the world within and the world without.[3] But the human form of Jehovah has disappeared, and the sun or halo behind his head has expanded till it fills the whole heavens, and spreads into the "unknown" beyond the margin of the design.[4] It still corresponds to Job, however, and represents a phase of his life. For in response to Job's advancing

[1] Job xlii. 8.
[2] Cp. Illus. 2, 5, 9, 13, 14, 15, 16 & 17.
[3] "What is Above is Within" ("J^m.", p. 71, l. 6).
[4] "There is an Outside spread Without, & an Outside spread Within
Beyond the Outline of Identity both ways, which meet in One:"
("J^m.", p. 18, ll. 2, 3.)

ILLUSTRATION XVIII   121

left foot, it shows four great rays on the right-hand side of its disk
(*i.e.*, where the Deity's right foot would be if he were portrayed in
human form), as against only three on its left.   This feature of the
Divine Light is so marked as to be felt even on earth.   On one
side we see a glow over the horizon behind the hills, and light
shines between the trunks of the trees in the middle distance, while
on the other side the horizon is dark, and the trees shut out the
light.   Job's wife, too, is in light ; while the friends on the
other side are in shade.   Job has now himself become the Divine
Image, and the Heavenly light is his own state of mind become
visible.   For—

> " In Great Eternity, every particular Form gives forth or Emanates
>   Its own peculiar Light, & the Form is the Divine Vision
>   And the Light is his Garment.   This is Jerusalem in every Man,
>   A Tent & Tabernacle of Mutual Forgiveness." [1]

And just as the impersonal sun represents Job's indwelling
divine life, so I cannot doubt that the pure flame represents the
purged Satanic element in him.   In the " Last Judgment " design
(Illus. 16), Satan and the Satanic Job and wife were shown falling
out of their enveloping flame, not *with* it, like Satan in Illus. 5.
The flame itself rises as it opens below to cast its evil burden into
the greedy abyss of annihilation.   And here we probably have the
same flame representing the regenerate human will, drawn irresis-
tibly up from its stony altar into the " Bosom of God, the Human

---

[1] " J^m.", p. 54, ll. 1-4.
  Cp. " Man is adjoind to Man by his Emanative portion :
      Who is Jerusalem in every individual Man . . .

. . . .
      O search & see : turn your eyes inward : open O thou World
      Of Love & Harmony in Man : expand thy ever lovely Gates."
                                             (" J^m.", p. 44, ll. 38-42.)

Imagination."[1] For the Will is, according to Blake, primarily "evil" or "hell," being, as he believes, essentially selfish.[2] But where it freely submits itself to the service of the indwelling Poetic Genius or Divine-Humanity, and recognises that this is the source of all its good, "Good & Evil are here both Good, & the two contraries Married."[3]

It was an after-thought of Blake's to represent Job with his back to the Spectator.[4] By so doing he makes the correspondence of Job's left side with his Deity's right into a unison ; the more illumined half of the design containing both.   And in this way he symbolises the fact that Job, in the very act of humbling himself as man, is exalted to identity with God.   Unlike his act of charity in Illus. 5, where the gift of a material thing was conceived by him as a spiritual act, here the spiritual act of surrendering his individual

[1] " J^m.", p. 5, l. 20.

[2] " There can be no Good Will, Will is always Evil . . . to others." (These words appear clearly amidst much that is illegible on the fly-leaf of Blake's copy of Swedenborg's " Angelic Wisdom " in the British Museum).

[3] " Swed.," p. 56 (misquoted by Ellis, " God and evil are here both good, etc.," Ellis, p. 110).
The idea of the good and evil aspects working together and being reconciled, is, of course, the theme of the " Marriage of Heaven and Hell," and occurs in " J^m.", p. 8, ll. 39-40, and 27, v. 19 and 83, ll. 78, 79.

[4] Gilchrist, ii. p. 214. This correspondence of Job and Jehovah here depicted opens a deeply-interesting chapter in Blake's symbolism, which, however, can only be cursorily touched on. It has been suggested that his mythic name " Los," is the reverse of Sol (Russell, p. 110 note), and in a poem in a letter to Thos. Butts (22nd Nov. 1802, Russell, p. 111), he says: " 'Twas outward a Sun, inward Los in his might." As all his engraved works had to be written and cut on the plate reversed, it seems possible that he sometimes conceived himself as *within* the page facing the spectator or reader, and thus came to look upon reversed writing as more inward, which would explain his choosing the word " Los " as the name of his most important mythic personage. In " Jerusalem " and " Milton," several important mottoes, written across the designs, are in reversed writing, and he may have conceived Hebrew as having a special sanctity in connection with its being written right to left. *Vide* also Appendix A on right and left symbolism.

ILLUSTRATION XVIII 123

will on behalf of his friends, is done in perfect humility as that of an earthly man for his earthly brethren, for "Attempting to be more than man we become less."[1] The same idea is repeated in the position of Job's wife, who exchanges her usual place upon Job's right for his left, and thereby finds herself on the Divine right. Her cramped and diminished figure is no doubt expressive of extreme humility, and is one of Blake's less fortunate attempts to express emotions in his attitudes.

In this spirit of self-offering Blake shows his own palette and brushes in the margin, and the long unfolding scroll of his writings. He here offers up the labours of his brush and pen to the Poetic Genius[2] on behalf of a world that mistook his gold for dross, in the prayer that there may be some who shall thereby be spared the bitterness of his own descent into the pit. For though genius makes its own way through the darkness, there has always been a majority of mankind, "who, though willing, were too weak to reject error without the assistance and countenance of those already in the truth : for a man can only reject error by the advice of a friend, or by the immediate inspiration of God."[3]

The Angels in the margin show, though less distinctly, the same motion as those on the title-page. The open Scriptures beneath speak of forgiveness as leading to the perfection of God, who " maketh his Sun to shine on the Evil & the Good."

[1] " F. Z." ("Vala," ix. l. 706).
[2] *Cp.* "Christianity is Art " (" Laocoon "), and
" The Glory of Christianity is, To Conquer by Forgiveness." ("Jᵐ.", p. 52.)
[3] " V. L. J." (Gilchrist, ii. p. 197).

19

The Lord maketh Poor & maketh Rich.

He bringeth Low & Lifteth Up

who provideth for the
Raven his Food
When his young ones cry unto God

Every one also gave him a piece of Money

Who remembered us in our low estate
For his Mercy endureth for ever

W Blake inv & sculp

London Published as the Act directs March 8 1825 by William Blake 3 Fountain Court Strand

ILLUSTRATION XIX

"All Things Common." Laocoon.

THIS design corresponds in certain aspects to the fourth, where Job and his wife sat under their tree and received the messengers of disaster. Here the messengers of mercy come, and though the flocks of sheep are gone, a humbler prosperity seems to have returned with the fruits and cornfields. In another aspect it corresponds to the fifth, where Job gives to the beggar. Blake was quick to perceive the difference between Job's position now and before his disasters. For where he used to give, he must now receive. It is the earthly man's last trial, and one to which Blake himself was keenly alive.[1] And yet these givers are very different from Job when he gave to the beggar. Though from the material point of view their sacrifice is incomparably less, yet in their complete freedom from ideas of merit, they are nearer the true wisdom of humanity. They give with a kind humility, that makes Job's trial as light as possible.[2] But it is always easier for a proud man to give than to receive, and when we see Job's extreme difficulty in accepting from anyone, however kindly sympathetic, we see why, even when he shared his last meal with the beggar, he had

---

[1] "I ordered of him to-day a copy of his songs for 5 guineas—My manner of receiving his mention of price pleased him—He spoke of his horror of money and of turning pale when it was offered him—and this was certainly unfeigned." "H. C. R Rem.," 19th Feb. 1826 (Symons, p. 303); *cp.* "H. C. R. Diary," 18th Feb. 1826 (Symons, p. 268).

[2] One is reminded of Linnell and his family. Surely no patron ever had a more tender and delicate acknowledgment than this design.

still to go through such severe trials of Experience before Satan
lost all hold upon him.

When one considers how much of Blake's own life-story must
be in these pictures, there seems a special beauty in his representing
the only ideal and wholly lovable act of material "benevolence"
as the one in which his hero was not the donor but the recipient.

The palm-trees in the margin probably signify the prosperity
of the righteous. "The righteous shall flourish like the palm
tree."[1] The text quoted immediately below the design, is an
instance of Blake's giving only an extract from the passage he
illustrates. The complete text should be "Every man also gave
him a piece of money, and every one an earring of gold."[2] For
the wife of Job's benefactor is giving Job's wife not a coin but an
ornament of some kind.

[1] Ps. xcii. 12.   [2] Job xlii. 11.

20

How precious are thy thoughts
unto me O God
how great is the sum of them

There were not found Women fair as the Daughters of Job

in all the Land & their Father gave them Inheritance

among their Brethren

If I ascend up into Heaven thou art there
If I make my bed in Hell behold Thou
art there

London Published as the Act directs March 8 1825 by William Blake N 3 Fountain Court Strand

ILLUSTRATION XX

"To speak to future generations by a sublime allegory." Letter to Thos. Butts, 6th July 1803.

THIS Illustration shows us what Blake would call the Christian life; the life of artistic productivity. "Christianity is Art," he says, and again, "A Poet a Painter a Musician an Architect, the Man Or Woman who is not one of these is not a Christian"; "Prayer is the Study of Art, Praise is the Practise of Art."[1]

Job is now regenerate, and his daughters sit round him listening to his great "Song of Experience,"[2] the typical episodes of which we may see graven on the walls behind.[3] The panel on Job's right tells of the dire deeds of man against man; the panel on his left of the disasters Nature inflicts—both inspired by Satan.[4] In the

[1] All from the "Laocoon." But in "Jerusalem" (p. 77), he includes what he calls "Science" and all intellectual pursuits: "Let every Christian, as much as in him lies engage himself openly & publicly before all the World in some Mental pursuit for the Building up of Jerusalem."

[2] In a pencil note on the fly-leaf of Blake's copy of Swedenborg's "Angelic Wisdom," a few words stand out clear amidst general obliteration. Amongst these are the words, " Suffering and Distress, *i.e.* Experience"—the first part of the sentence probably being "Understanding [is in no way natural to] Man it is acquired by means of Suffering and Distress, *i.e.* Experience." *Cp.* also the quotation from the " Four Zoas," *supra* p. 12 (*cp.* "Vala," ii. ll. 397-418).

[3] *Cp.* " All things acted on Earth are seen in the bright Sculptures of
   Los's Halls & every Age renews its powers from these Works
   With every pathetic story possible to happen from Hate or
   Wayward Love & every sorrow & distress is carved here
   Every Affinity of Parents, Marriages & Friendships are here
   In all their various combinations wrought with wondrous Art
   All that can happen to Man in his pilgrimage of seventy years."
                                        ("Jm.", p. 16, ll. 61-67.)

[4] The distinction is not in the Book of Job. Blake's distinction seems, therefore, to be significant (Job i. 13-19).

127

centre we see the whirlwind that passes over the heads of Job's friends, but pours its full blast upon himself and his wife, and yet in so doing reveals to them the present Deity.[1]

Beneath are the vaults of those who still sleep in the grave of unregenerate life, but whom his story shall call forth to life indeed.[2] "By words which speak of nothing more than what we are, would I arouse the sensual from their sleep of death, and win the vacant and the vain to noble raptures," says Wordsworth in the great fragment about the human mind and the external world first printed in his Preface to the "Excursion," and so much admired by Blake that he made at least two manuscript copies of it.[3]

[1] Crabb Robinson (Symons, p. 259) says of Blake· "Tho' he spoke of his happiness, he spoke of past sufferings, and of sufferings as necessary—'There is suffering in Heaven, for where there is the capacity of enjoyment, there is the capacity of pain'" (10th Dec. 1825). *Cp.* "H. C. R. Rem" (Symons, p. 291).

Gilchrist tells a beautiful story (1. p. 353) of his saying to a lovely child of wealthy parents: "May God make this world to you, my child, as beautiful as it has been to me!" *Cf.* poem written at the end of his MS. book, and, therefore, probably, towards the end of his life (Sampson, p 238). "I rose up at the dawn of day," etc. (extract quoted *supra*, page 12).

[2] *Cp.* "J^m.", p. 96, ll. 38, 39, where Albion's Son & Daughters awake from their sleep.

[3] "H. C. R. Diary," 18th Feb. 1826 (Symons, p. 266); but *cp.* the Reminiscences (p. 298), where an obviously different MS. copy is referred to. *Cp.* also reference to a copy in H. C. R.'s Letter to D. Wordsworth (Symons, p. 275). In spite of his admiration for the lines, Blake could not endure the passage :—

> "For I must tread on shadowy ground, must sink
> Deep—and, aloft ascending, breathe in worlds
> To which the heaven of heavens is but a veil.
> All strength—all terror, single or in bands,
> That ever was put forth in personal form ;
> Jehovah, with his thunder, and the choir
> Of shouting angels, and the empyreal thrones,
> I pass them, unalarm'd."

"What does he mean by 'the worlds to which the heaven of heavens is but a

ILLUSTRATION XX   129

Perhaps we may think of the sleepers as Job's sons, who met their spiritual death in Illus. 3 (where it will be remembered the daughters did not appear, but only the sons' wives),[1] and appear in the next illustration risen with their sisters and parents into the regenerate life. This would certainly make a more satisfying conclusion than the complete new family Job is represented as begetting in the Bible.

The exaggeration of some of the limbs in this design, especially the left arm of the daughter kneeling before Job, is an unfortunate attempt to emphasise the active nature of the "New Church."[2] Job's outspread hands recall the attitude of the indwelling Creator in Illus. 14, and it is not impossible that the daughters represent the sun, the moon and the earth, as symbolically used in that design beneath the Deity's right hand, left hand and feet respectively. This would further account for the extreme solidity of the middle daughter, whose head is turned to her left. The beauty and symmetry of the silhouette is strikingly brought out by holding the design upside down and half-closing the eyes.

In the margin, the vines and grapes probably symbolise Christ and Christian joy, and the musical instruments, Art.

veil,' and who is he that shall 'pass Jehovah unalarmed?'" Crabb Robinson's letter to Dorothy Wordsworth (Symons, p. 275).

Although it was certainly unreasonable, it is easy to understand Blake's objection to these passages. For Blake had chosen the very images and symbols which Wordsworth here rejects, to express what Wordsworth had to say. Blake's Jehovah and his choir of shouting angels (Illus. 14 of this book) is Wordsworth's "discerning intellect of man when wedded to this goodly universe in love and holy passion . . . and the creation (by no lower name can it be called) which they with blended might accomplish."

[1] *Vide supra* Illus. 3, p. 55.

[2] "The Whole of the New Church is in the Active Life & not in ceremonies at all" ("Swed.," p. 181).

I

21

Great & Marvellous are thy Works Lord God Almighty

Just & True are thy Ways O thou King of Saints

So the Lord blessed the latter end of Job
more than the beginning

After this Job lived
an hundred & forty years
& saw his Sons & his
Sons Sons

even four Generations
So Job died
being old
& full of days

In burnt Offerings for Sin
thou hast had no Pleasure

W Blake inv & sculp

London Published as the Act directs March 8 1825 by William Blake No 3 Fountain Court Strand

ILLUSTRATION XXI

"For lo! the Night of Death is past and the Eternal Day
Appears upon our Hills: Awake Jerusalem." ("Jm.", p. 97, ll. 3, 4.)

And here the story ends. The long night is over, and the sun which was setting in the first Illustration now rises again upon Job's life.

Before turning to the design itself, a piece of symbolism in the margin will sum up for us the whole story and tell us in one word the change made in Job's life. The marginal design of the first Illustration corresponds with this one, except for the text on the altar and the reversed positions of the bullock and ram. These, I believe, though I have been unable to verify the fact, symbolise respectively Innocence and Experience, in which case their altered position is full of meaning. In the first design the bull is "experience," seated in the spiritual or imaginative side of the design, and the ram is "innocence," established in the corporeal side. In other words, Job's "experience" is as yet merely imaginative, not corporeal as it is to become: whereas his "innocence" or happiness resides in his corporeal prosperity. But now he has "fixed" and "corporealised" earthly experience in all its bitterness, by which means alone he can learn to "cast it off" and at the same time to find the impregnable seat of true "innocence" in the "Bosom of God, the Human Imagination." Innocence based on bodily good was unstable; experience in imagination was inadequate.[1] But experience embodied, enables man to reject the unreality of the flesh and the earth, and to save its eternal innocence.[2]

Accordingly in the design itself we see Job now regenerate, his left hand raised to offer up his redeemed corporeal man in

[1] *Cp.* "What is the price of experience? Do men buy it for a song?" "F. Z." ("Vala," ii. 397).

[2] *Cp.* "All Life is Holy," "Lav." 299 (Ellis, p. 133), with "Energy is the only life and is from the Body" ("M. H. H.," p. 4). *Vide* also Illus. 12 *supra*, p. 91 *ff.*

service of the eternal spirit;[1] while with right hand he plays his
psaltery of praise.[2]   On his right stands his wife, older but more
beautiful for all she has endured.   As symbolically shown, she still
reigns over all that is corporeal in Man in complement to Job.   Only
twice throughout the book has her right foot appeared.   Once when
she supported her husband's feet after Satan had driven all light
from his face,[3] and again when she detected Job's error of self-
righteousness in the tenth Illustration.   But she has nearly always
been on Job's right side, for to him she has been a spirit.[4]   "You
have ever been an angel to me,"[5] said Blake to his own wife on his
death-bed—but she was the kind of angel who through forty-five
years of discouragement and difficulty, could keep the earthly home
sweet and dignified[6] for a man "so little with her, though in the body
they were never separated; for he was incessantly away in Paradise."[7]

And now the instruments of music are taken down from the
tree; the words below tell of the passing of the ceremonial law
into the gospel of spiritual joy and freedom; while Job's risen
family raise their spiritual symphony to mingle with the song of
the morning stars, as the rising sun engulfs their light.

[1] *Cp.* Illus. 18.
[2] *Cp.* Illus. 20.   "Praise is the Practise of Art" ("Laocoon").
[3] Illus. 6.
[4] *Vide supra* Illus. 2, p. 53.   Also App F. on the "Creation of Eve," p. 145.
[5] So Gilchrist (vol. i. p. 404), except for the inversion of the third and fourth
words, quoting perhaps (though inexactly) from Cunningham's "Life" (Symons, p
429).   So also Tatham in his account recorded in a footnote in J T. Smith's
"Memoirs" (Symons, p. 379).   But, curiously, enough, Tatham's own version in
his "Life" is more prosaic—"Kate, you have been a good wife" (Russell, p. 35).
For a similar idea in Blake's own writings, however, *cp.* "J^m.", p. 14, ll. 13, 14 :—
      "Enitharmon is a vegetated mortal Wife of Los.
      His Emanation, yet his Wife till the sleep of death is past."
[6] Gilchrist, i. ch. 34, esp., pp. 349 and 358.
[7] Swinburne, p. 81 note (Mr. Seymour Kirkup's reminiscences), also quoted by
Gilchrist (i. p. 410).

APPENDIX A

THE explanation of the meaning of the right and left sides in Blake's pictures, and especially of the right and left feet, first occurred to me when considering his designs of "William" and "Robert" in the prophetic book "Milton." The very conspicuous position of William's left foot is emphasised by its being especially referred to in the text ("Mⁿ.", p. 14, l. 49), and this made it seem the more significant that in the reversed design of "Robert" the same foot becomes the right instead of the left. "William" and "Robert" are, of course, Blake and his dead brother (conceived as dwelling in the spirit).[1] There seemed strong *prima facie* reasons, therefore, for believing that Blake pictured a correspondence between the right side of spiritual beings, or those in spiritual states ; and the left of those still in the flesh, or in a corporeal state.

In the Job this symbolism is considerably elaborated and refined, and used of the two aspects of the same individual, and although I have not been able to discover definitely what he meant by it in every case (what for instance is the exact meaning of the feet of the sons and daughters in the last design. Probably they are in some way complementary to one another and to Job),[2] it is clear that the feet and hands practically always mean *something*, and generally something very clear and relevant to the subject as conceived by Blake.

How early in his life Blake worked out the system we find here I cannot say. In "Songs of Innocence," "The Marriage of Heaven and Hell" and "The Songs of Experience," it seems to be definitely absent

[1] "Thirteen years ago I lost a brother, and with his spirit I converse daily and hourly in the spirit, and see him in my remembrance, in the regions of my imagination." Letter to Wm. Hayley, 6th May 1800 (Russell, pp. 68, 69).

[2] The sons on Job's right are all right but one, the sons on his left, all left but one ; the daughter on his right is left, the one in the centre both right and left, but the one on his left shows no foot, for evidently for a woman to show right foot only (which would make the design symmetrical) is something very grievous. Job's wife only does so in Illustration 6, *q.v.*, especially note 1 (p. 73).

133

(*e.g.*, Christ is left in heaven, "Little Black Boy," or is he possibly come to earth?) In "Urizen," "America" and "Europe," it seems to be used of the Zoas sometimes, Los being prevailingly left and Urizen right, though (perhaps for some reason) not consistently.[1] But when we come to the "Milton" it is used both of Los and Urizen (p. 15); of Ololon and probably Satan (p. 8), and of Milton, Blake and his brother. Milton is left as he descends to earth (p. 13); Los is left as he steps from his solar chariot (p. 21); Ololon (p. 36) is left as she descends into Blake's garden, Blake is always left himself (pp. 14, 19, 29, 36), and the central figure on the last page is left in the "stems of vegetation." On the other hand, Milton is right on the title-page and in his redemptive act on p. 41, and Robert is right (p. 33). In "Jerusalem," I can find nothing to definitely prove either its absence or presence.[2] In many of his paintings and drawings he seems to use it. To take a single example, in his "Christ in the house of Martha and Mary" (called "But Martha was cumbered about much serving," Gilchrist ii. p. 239), Christ shows right hand and foot only, Martha is left foot only (right hand less prominent), and Mary both;[3] but with the right hand and right foot moved into an unnatural position, so as to be the more conspicuous. Blake's use of the right and left feet in the

---

[1] The well-known frontispiece to the "Europe," called "The Ancient of Days" or the "Act of Creation," appears to use the symbolism (and it is the more conspicuous because it shows the figure of Urizen, who is usually right, with left hand and foot advanced). Here the "Creator" rolls round the compasses which define existence, *with his left hand*, for (like the Deity in Illus. 15 of this series) he is creating the transitory world. It therefore seems to illustrate the passage in "Jerusalem":—

". . . I saw the finger of God go forth

. . . . . .

Fixing their Systems, permanent : by mathematic power

Giving a body to Falsehood that it may be cast off for ever" ("Jm", p. 12, ll. 10-13)

cp. also another conception of Creation on p. 14 of "Urizen" where the left hand is used by another Zoa.

[2] As there are no earthly characters in the book (like Blake in the "Milton" or Job in the "Job"), the symbolism, if used at all, may be used with a somewhat different significance I notice, however, that Jerusalem (like Job's wife) is always left, and Los prevailingly right, as is also Albion in regeneration The key is perhaps to be found in the great crucifixion design frontispiece to chap iv., where a correspondence and unison between Albion and Christ is attained in exactly the opposite way from that between Job and his Deity (Illus. 18). That is to say, Jerusalem is the story of God becoming Man, as Job is the story of Man becoming God—and as Los is the spiritual or universal man in his bodily aspect, so Job's story is of the spiritual aspect of an earthly man.

[3] Note, again, woman's right must not appear alone (*cp.* note 2, p. 133, present Appendix).

"Paradise Lost" designs (nearly contemporary with the "Job"), is clearly systematic, as may be seen by the table below (Appendix B).

There are not many references in the writings to the association of the left side with the earthly, and the right with the spiritual or imaginative. "Jerusalem" and the "Four Zoas" each have a reference to the left hand, which perhaps confirms but would certainly not establish the symbolism.

Left Hand. "So saying she took a Falshood & hid it in her left hand" ("J^m.", p. 82, l. 17). This falsehood was .

"But if you on Earth Forgive
You shall not find where to Live" ("J^m.", p. 81, text in Illus. in reversed writing).

"Now my left hand I stretch abroad, even to Earth beneath." "F. Z." ("Vala," ii. l. 369).

All the other references are from the "Milton," and are as follows :—
Right Hand. "Daughters of Beulah ! Muses who inspire the Poet's Song

. . Come into my hand
By your mild power : descending down the Nerves of my right arm
From out the Portals of my Brain, where by your ministry
The Eternal Great Humanity Divine, planted his Paradise"
("Mⁿ.", p. 3, ll. 1-8).

This passage seems as though it might have suggested the whole of this symbolism.

Left Foot. "Upon his fibrous left Foot black : most dismal to our eyes"
(*Ibid.*, p. 20, l. 35).
"And all this Vegetable World appeard on my left Foot" (*Ibid.*, p 19, l. 12).

But the most interesting and important passage confirming the right and left symbolism, at first appears to confute it. It is as follows :—
"The Souls descending to the Body, wail on the right hand
Of Los : & those deliverd from the Body, on the left hand."

This is explained by the next line :—
"For Los against the east his force continually bends" (*Ibid.*, p. 26, ll. 16-18).

Now the East, as we know from a passage in "Jerusalem," is "Inwards" ("J^m.", p. 14, l. 31), and although even so the statement remains somewhat cryptic, it suggests that Los is pictured as standing with his back to the spectator and his face *inwards*, in which case his right and left would be the same as Job's in Illustration 18 (*vide supra* note 2, p. 134 and note 4, p. 122, Illus. 18), and *opposite* to the divine right and left, as shown in that and other Illustrations. In this case the above passage would be equivalent to the statement, "those descending to the body are on the left side of Jehovah (or Christ), and those delivered on the right," which is, of course, the fact in all the "Last Judgment" pictures. Fortunately, there is an Illustration in the "Four Zoas" manuscript (the first of the "Vala" Illustrations reproduced by E. & Y.) which puts the matter beyond doubt. Here we see Los (identified by having the sun on his head) standing with back to the spectator, while one figure descends on his right side, another sleeps by his right foot, a third wakes by his left foot and a fourth rises upon his left side, thus preserving the clockwise motion and establishing the fact that the right and left sides of Los are here the opposite of the Divine right and left, from which the symbolism is derived.

It is further interesting in this connection to note that Los is three times in "Jerusalem" (pp. 1, 62[1] and 73) represented with back to the spectator, and also elsewhere in the prophetic books (notably title-page "Bk. of Los"), whereas I can find only one clear case of any of the other Zoas being so represented ("Urizen," p. 25). On the other hand, it seems highly significant that at the end of "Jerusalem" the regenerate *Albion* is thrice (pp. 76, 95 and 97) represented with back to the spectator. That is to say, when the Zoas became re-united in him, it is Los's inward attitude that has at last prevailed, securing the unison of the corporeal and divine referred to in Illustration 18, and probably "Jerusalem," p. 76 (*vide supra* note 2, p. 134, present Appendix).

[1] Where a diminutive "Los" looks *inwards*, gazing at a Titanic figure of the "natural" sun, looking *outwards*, in agony, and wreathed in the Serpent's folds (the Serpent symbolises Nature, *vide supra* note 3, p. 88, etc.)

After the above was already in type I found myself obliged to revise my opinion as to the absence of this symbolism in the early works. In "M. H. H.," at all events, it is almost certainly used. In one illustration the feet were placed so conspicuously and in a way that seemed so definitely to contradict the preceding designs, that I abandoned the idea of there being a consistent system in the work. I am now satisfied that I had mistaken Hell for Heaven in this design—possibly a pardonable error but a sufficient one

APPENDIX B

I APPEND a table which may help the reader in the designs to Milton's
" Paradise Lost."

God the Father (only seen in heaven), God the Son, and Raphael and
Michael (only seen on earth) are right in heaven and left on earth. God
the Son is also "left" when he drives out of heaven in his chariot
("Paradise Lost," bk. vi. l. 750, top of p. 199 in Liverpool Booksellers'
Edition) against the rebel host.[1]

Eve always shows both feet, but the left is more advanced, except where
she sleeps under the cross, and here she is an "inward" vision rather than a
"vegetated" woman, as indicated by her being separated off from the rest
of the scene in her symbolic bower (*vide infra* Appendix F).

Adam also always shows both feet, but has the right more advanced
until Eve yields to temptation, after which he remains left until the vision
of the Crucifixion.

Satan is always right in the presence of man or devils, but left in the
presence of God the Son.

[1] In the Illustration of Christ judging Adam and Eve, neither foot is uncovered, though the right
leg is more advanced. This is clearly because it would be unsuitable to represent him as "left" when
giving a spiritual judgment, and yet he cannot be represented "right" when upon earth

APPENDIX C

Symbolism of the Diurnal Motion

CONSIDERING the important place it took in his thoughts, there are comparatively few passages in Blake's works which conclusively show that he regarded the diurnal motion as symbolical. The passage quoted above from the poem on p. 77 of "Jerusalem" stands almost alone.[1] There is, however, sufficient evidence in the designs alone to establish it beyond a doubt. First a small design on p. 72 of "Jerusalem," in which this world is represented by a rocky disc or sphere, wept over by angels right and left, has a legend running *clockwise* round it as follows:—" Continually Building, Continually Decaying because of Love & Jealousy." With this should be compared a similar design on p. 54, where the clockwise motion is shown by the small figures right and left of the disc. These are merely confirmations. More important and interesting is the fact that the myth both in " Jerusalem " and the " Four Zoas " is connected with the diurnal motion, as Messrs. Ellis and Yeats have shown. In the " Four Zoas," this is very clear, as it expressly begins with sunset ("F. Z." *cp.* " Vala," i. l. 20), and concludes with dawn ("F. Z." *cp.* " Vala," ix. l. 647 ; *cp. Ibid.*, ll. 391 *ff.*). Also the first symbolical design, reproduced in " Vala " E. & Y., iii., represents the sun in the centre and figures right and left, clearly showing the clockwise motion (*cp.* Appendix A, *vide supra* pp. 135, 6).

In " Jerusalem," also sunset and dawn begin and end the drama as indicated in three different ways. In the text the sunset does not actually occur till the beginning of chap. ii. (p. 29, ll. 1-2), but chap. i. may almost be regarded as a kind of prelude to the whole, in which the stories of Los and his sons and daughters, and of their labours for Jerusalem, prepare

---

[1] *Vide supra* p. 47 and note 4, *ibid.*

the way for the story of Albion proper. At the end of the poem the dawn is finely described as the rising of Albion ("J^m.", p. 95, ll. 5-15).

> " The Breath Divine went forth over the morning hills Albion rose
> In anger; the wrath of God breaking bright, flaming on all sides around
> His awful limbs ; into the Heavens he walked clothed in flames
> Loud thundring, with broad flashes of flaming lightning & pillars
> Of fire, speaking the Words of Eternity in Human Forms, in direful
> Revolutions of Action & Passion, thro the Four Elements on all sides
> Surrounding his awful Members. Thou seest the Sun in heavy clouds
> Struggling to rise above the Mountains, in his burning hand
> He takes his Bow, then chooses out his arrows of flaming gold
> Murmuring the Bowstring breathes with ardor ! clouds roll round the
> Horns of the wide Bow, loud sounding winds sport on the mountain brows."

and later ("J^m.", p. 97, ll. 1-4) :—

> "Awake Awake Jerusalem ! O lovely Emanation of Albion
> Awake and overspread all Nations as in Ancient Time
> For lo! the Night of Death is past, and the Eternal Day
> Appears upon our Hills : Awake Jerusalem, and come away "

In the Illustrations there is also conclusive evidence that the course of the drama follows the apparent solar cycle. It is probable that the Illustration on p. 6, of Los and his spectre, is representative of sunset.[1] Not only the strange beams or rays from the furnace, but, more significant, the iron chain descending on Los's left are suggestive of this—what is certain is that a sunrise is shown in the heading of the final chapter (chap. iv., "J^m.", p. 78) where the form of a man with a cock's head clearly symbolises " the bird of dawning," showing that the half-hidden sun he is watching is rising not setting. Lastly, the first and last pages of the work (1 and 100) are respectively of Los carrying a sun into the caverns of the underworld, and of his finally liberating one from night and the " Serpent temple," to be carried upwards by a figure on his right.

---

[1] If Los is here fronting "East" (*vide supra* pp. 135, 6), his back being to the " West," gives an additional reason for regarding the flame at his back as symbolical of sunset.

APPENDIX D

THE *Satanic (or more frequently the " Starry ") Wheels* [1] is Blake's name for those systems of thought which conceive the Universe upon a rationalistic basis—and with these he associates such Religious or Moral codes as base Society on penalties for wrong-doing. For the one attempts to make all think uniformly by coercive logic, the other to make all act uniformly by coercive law. In this way he conceives that all which is of supreme value, to wit spontaneous thought and action, is wounded and crushed ("Jᵐ.", p. 15, ll. 14-20).

> " I turn my eyes to the Schools & Universities of Europe
>   And there behold the Loom of Locke whose Woof rages dire
>   Washd by the Water-wheels of Newton, black the cloth
>   In heavy wreathes folds over every Nation : cruel Works
>   Of many Wheels I view, wheel without wheel, with cogs tyrannic
>   Moving by compulsion each other : not as those in Eden : which
>   Wheel within Wheel in freedom revolve in harmony & peace."

The freedom of the " Wheels " of Eden is connected with his doctrine of the Essence and Identities (*vide* Illus. 17 and Appendix E). Identities are all free and independent, being united only in Essence. They are never identically one, but may become essentially one in love. If we were each mere wheels or externally connected fragments of a single identity, " Heaven would upon this plan be but a Clock " [2]—the absence or imperfection of any one part would destroy the Whole. But being one in essence, the essence may be perfect in each individual and is not to be lost so long as it is preserved in any one, while it may yet be repeated without limit, in innumerable men and things.

On p. 22 of "Jerusalem" is a design in which we see three gigantic cog-wheels setting behind a boundless sea into an abyss of flame. Above these and repeating their undulations is a chain of angels. Over each wheel a pair [3] of angels makes an arch with joined hands, and each pair is linked to the next with feet and wings. This design appears to symbolise the two ways of conceiving the nexus of the universe or of weaving its facts into a whole ; as expressed by the text above.

> " Why should Punishment Weave the Veil with Iron Wheels of War
>   When Forgiveness might it Weave with Wings of Cherubim." [4]

---

[1] " Jᵐ.", p. 5, l. 4, etc , etc., etc.
[3] Only one pair can be fully seen.
[2] " Swed.", p. 24.
[4] *Cp.* also design of " Jᵐ.", p. 75.

APPENDIX E

(Additional Note to Illustration 17)

As readers interested in these questions will have noticed, Blake's alternating vision of contraction and expansion, is a method of basing a religious or emotional Monism, on a genuine philosophic Pluralism.

For Blake himself, the scheme is associated with his conceptions of Christ and Christianity, and with certain characteristic ideas about "forgiveness" and "imagination." But the subject is so interesting that I will ask leave to give a free rendering of the scheme as it appears to emerge when divested of its poetic and symbolic setting.

In Nature, Blake finds nothing which we ought to dignify by the name of Unity—though the material scientist finds a kind of blind necessity which he mistakes for unity.[1] To worship this is the error of the Deist[2]—not to say the Atheist. We need not necessarily assert, indeed, that Blake rejects outward nature *ontologically*, as is often urged, and as many of his utterances certainly suggest.[3] What is indisputable is that he rejects external nature as the seat of Deity;—except perhaps in the last resort, and then because the Divine light is inextinguishable even in the deepest abyss. To him Nature is at best a "fortuitous

---

[1] "Jm.", p. 15, ll. 14-20, quoted *supra* p 140, etc.   [2] "Jm", p. 52, etc.
[3] "H. C. R. Diary" (Symons, p. 259) : "Every thing is *Atheism* which assumes the reality of the Natural & Unspiritual world." Also (Symons, p. 263). "He denied that the natural world is any thing It is all nothing and Satan's empire is the empire of nothing"; and (Symons, p. 265)· "Nature is the work of the Devil" On the other hand, such sayings as "The Devil is in us, as far as we are Nature," prove that Nature did *actually* exist for Blake and had some part in us Moreover, the appearance of the "Non Ens" itself, "seen in regeneration terrific or complacent varying according to the subject of discourse" in the finale of Jerusalem ("Jm.", p. 98, ll. 33-35), would be gratuitous (not to say impossible) if "nonentity" was for Blake the same as being actually "not there." I cannot resist the conviction that Blake's repudiation of Nature is moral and not strictly ontological—though how far he himself would have admitted this is another question.

concourse of incoherent, discordant principles of Love & Hate."[1]   He
is therefore driven to seek his unifying principle in Man.   But Man must
be no mere abstract idea.   It must be in real men that we find our unity
or not at all[2]—and here the real difficulty occurs, for the more we are
in touch with actual living men, the more obstinately do they appear to
be distinct and plural.   We may picture Blake himself, for instance,
delightfully certain that *his* identity was not a thing to be merged in any
other man's, human or divine.   And consistency led him to insist on the
same liberty of identity for others.   For the moment then, his resort to
Man seems to have removed his Unity further than ever.   And it is in
his method of overcoming this difficulty that he shows his admirable
sanity of mind.   His escape is found not in denying the facts of plurality,
which he continually re-asserts, but in spiritualising the conception of
Unity.   After all, the unity of contact and inclusion is not the highest,
and when we cease to look to the material world for our unity, we must
rise above mechanical and material conceptions of unity.[3]

Tangibly then, and even conceptually, we must admit men to be
necessarily and for ever individual and plural.   Yet there does exist, as the
greatest men have always felt, a profound, albeit purely spiritual, unity,
amongst us all, and it is through this that the ultimate unity of the universe
itself must be found.   This unity is not to be discovered by comparing,
relating and generalising a number of human beings and so losing their
distinctive individualities.[4]   All such intellectualisations of Man as an
objective phenomenon are futile.   What we must do is to go inwards and
examine the ultimate essence of our own conscious existence.   We then
learn that the essence as it dwells in ourselves is active consciousness
(Imagination) and desire (which must be chastened into the higher "love")
—this is what *we* are, and yet it is by applying this most immediate
and inward of all conceptions to other individuals, that we most nearly

[1] "F. Z.", *cp.* "Vala," ii. ll. 102, 3.   [2] "Jm.", p. 91, etc.
[3] *Ibid.*, p. 91, ll. 26-28, *cp.* "Swed.", p. 24, etc.
[4] *Ibid.*, p. 91, ll. 26-28 :—

    " You accumulate Particulars, & murder by analyzing, that you
      May take the aggregate   .   .   .   .   .   .
      And you call that Swelld & bloated Form a Minute Particular."

bridge the gulf that separates us from them. The innermost humanity, which makes each man an inviolable identity, *is* the supreme fact common to every human life. This is what Blake calls "God," the "intellectual" (as opposed to the external or materialistic) "fountain of Humanity."[1] It exists nowhere but in individual men—yet, wherever it exists, it is *the* supreme fact and essentially the *same* fact. It is doubly unifying—firstly because it is the same (essentially the same, not identically)[2] in every man ; and secondly, because in its supreme phase of love it breaks down the conflicting interests which our inalienable external plurality admits and even fosters.

It is from the vantage-ground of this conception of the universal human essence that we must re-interpret and re-unify Nature itself. Every creature and even every atom has its own loves and hates, which we must interpret by ours—and though the result is sometimes painful and even horrifying to the imagination (as exemplified as early as the "Book of Thel") it is the only way to find God in the outward order.

In proposing the above as the most workable anatomy of Blake's system, I do not suggest that he had thought it out all precisely in the form here put. Neither do I for a moment suggest that it is something quite peculiar to Blake. Least of all do I propose it as an entirely practical system or ideal. I confess, however, that it does appear to me to have real value as suggesting a *mode* of unity which, without outraging the perpetual consciousness of actual plurality to which the mind is subject, yet helps to assuage the human demand for some form of Monism, while showing a very sane appreciation of the true direction in which we must seek the realisation of human unity.

Moreover, if not explicit, it is, I believe, implicit in all Blake's highest flights of thought, and until we have grasped it, we miss the innerness of almost all his best. The matter may be concluded here by a characteristic example, which shows very clearly his anxiety to preserve in every conception both his spiritual Monism and his intellectual Pluralism.

[1] "Jm.", p. 91, l. 10.
[2] *Cp.* "N. N. R. (b)" : "As all men are alike in outward form So (*and with the same infinite variety*) all are alike in the Poetic Genius." (Italics mine.)

In the great passage quoted on the Dedication-page of this book, he says :

> " When in Eternity Man converses with Man they enter
> Into each others Bosom (which are Universes of delight)."[1]

Bosom is here intentionally put in the singular and universes in the plural, to counteract the natural tendency of the mind to conceive two men's bosoms as necessarily plural, and the universe common to both as necessarily singular. Blake holds that the contrary is equally true. All depends on the mode of vision. If the vision is according to identities, not only has each man his own bosom, but each bosom is (or has) its own independent universe ; whereas, seen according to essence, all true universes are in *the* human bosom ; which is always essentially the same, whether in you or me or any man. And this is what Blake calls " the Bosom of God, the Human Imagination."[2]

[1] " Jm.", p. 88, ll. 3, 4.   [2] " Jm.", p. 5, l. 20.

APPENDIX F

The Creation of Eve

The subject of the place of woman in Blake's scheme is extremely interesting though somewhat complex. It is rendered the more difficult from the fact that as in other cases his changes of sentiment obscure the real consistency of his basal ideas.

For Blake, "Humanity" included both the male and the female elements, either of which was incomplete without the other.[1] But when, as in this world, the two are separated the male appears to be always regarded as representing the human type, though imperfectly. This leads to one of Blake's curious complexities of thought. The female is regarded either (a) as the ever-present token of man's lapse from Man—and of the fact that the earthly man is not the true and perfect Humanity (which, of course, the earthly woman is still less); or (b) as the vehicle in which is preserved and from which shall ultimately proceed the beauty and goodness which the earthly man lacks to make him perfect Man (or God).[2]

Woman, therefore, in herself everything piteous, and weak,[3] brings in complement to the corporeal male all earthly light and salvation.[4] She represents on the one hand the symbol and genius of the earthly life, and on the other hand the uplifting spirit who, like the "little Clod of Clay" ("S. of E.") "makes a heaven in hell's despair."

We may without, I think, overstraining the theory of the completely symbolical character of Blake's later designs, read the expression of these ideas in the two illustrations to "Paradise Lost" entitled the "Creation of Eve" and the "Vision of the Crucifixion."

---

[1] "Jm.", p. 90, ll. 1, 2.
[2] The contrast between the isolated male and the male united with the female in Beulah is finely drawn in "Jm.", p. 69, ll. 1-30. Beulah, however, is here shown as an unstable condition.
[3] Urizen, pp. 16, 17, etc., etc.
[4] Cp. "Jm.", p. 55, ll. 1, 2.

The problem of this former design is to explain why Eve is created by the second and not the first person of the Trinity. The answer is, I suggest, as follows. Adam, who is fallen in death-like slumber, upon a great leaf symbolising the earthly or "Vegetative" life, has thereby destroyed the perfect image of the divine life in himself. This calls down the Eternal and Universal Humanity (always symbolised by Christ) to restore the loss; for it is impossible for man's Divinity to suffer eternal diminution. This restoration is achieved by evoking the human complement of the earthly (i.e. sleeping) male, in the female,[1] who is therefore in a sense the divinest part of man. And here Eve, as shown by the feet, is complementary to Adam. (The symbolism of Adam's and of Christ's feet has been suggested supra in Appendix B.)

In the prophetic Vision of the Crucifixion, we see the final and perfect redemption of the earthly Man achieved, by the death of Deity on the cross,[2] symbolising, one may suppose, the spiritualising of the vegetable (corporeal) life in its most acutely limited form. The cosmic tragedy— which from one point of view is a mere mutual annihilation of the supreme Divinity and the supreme Death—has, incidentally as it were, resulted in the creation of a form of ideal beauty, such as was alone capable of redeeming Earth from utter darkness, during the period of waiting for deliverance. But Eve, now no longer needed in the flesh—for man's complete nature has been restored and she is comprehended in Adam's being—remains as a pure vision, a potentiality of joy and beauty now realised by the perfect Humanity as eternally within itself, and seen as the inevitable outcome of the Crucifixion tragedy. And here Eve—detached from the actual scene, as a vision or emblem in her symbolic bower—is represented (by the feet) as complementary to, no longer the sleeping Adam, but, the slain Christ.

---

[1] Cp. "Jm.", p. 42. ll. 32-34.
        "But when Man sleeps in Beulah the Saviour in mercy takes
        Contractions Limit, and of the Limit he forms Woman : That
        Himself may in process of time be born Man to redeem."
[2] "Jesus replied, Fear not Albion : unless I die thou canst not live," "Jm.", p. 96, l. 14 ; cp. "Jm.", p. 90, l. 38 ; p. 62, ll. 18-20 ; p. 35, ll. 9, 10, etc.

APPENDIX G

SUMMARY OF THE STORY OF JOB

In the Bible Job is described as a man living in the land of Uz, and therefore not an Israelite. He is, however, a "perfect" man, and upright, one that feared God and eschewed evil. He possesses great wealth and a large family of sons and daughters, on whose behalf he is continually offering sacrifices, to guard against the consequences of some possible secret infidelity on their part. On a certain day, when Satan appears with the Sons of God before the Almighty, the Patriarch is instanced as a perfect man. Satan, however, suggests that his piety is dependent on his wealth, and that if he loses this he will renounce God. Accordingly Satan is allowed to put him to the test. But even after he has stripped him of all his possessions and slain all his children, Job says: "The Lord gave, and the Lord hath taken away; blessed be the name of the Lord." Still Satan challenges Job's disinterestedness; so long as the man himself escapes unscathed, he still has something to fear, and he worships God to save his "skin," "but put forth thine hand now, and touch his bone and his flesh, and he will curse thee to thy face." So Satan is allowed to go to any lengths short of actually killing the man, and he smites him "with sore boils from the sole of his foot unto his crown." Even Job's wife now fails him, and tells him to "curse God and die." "What?" says Job, "shall we receive good at the hand of God, and shall we not receive evil?" The three friends then appear, and for seven days sit by him in mute sympathy. At last Job breaks out into bitter lamentations over his undeserved fate. For this Eliphaz rebukes him, declaring that misfortune is never undeserved. Job answers him, and each of the friends in turn, but the more he persists in upholding his righteousness, the more vehement they become, and at last charge him recklessly with all manner of sins against his neighbour. "Is not thy wickedness great?" says Eliphaz in his third speech, "and thine iniquities infinite? For thou hast taken a pledge from thy brother for nought, and stripped the naked of their clothing." Job then appeals from man to God. Would that he could find the seat of the Almighty Himself, and there make his defence and "know the words which he would answer me." After this a fourth friend is introduced, Elihu, who insists that the power of God silences all question of his justice. Job is at all events wrong in appealing against the sentence of the Almighty and Inscrutable. Moreover, since God can have nothing to lose or gain by Job's actions, he cannot be motived by a vindictive spirit against him, and can only be influenced by pure justice. And now the great climax of the drama is reached, when the Deity himself appears in the whirlwind and charges Job with presumption —overwhelming him by the tale of his power and wisdom in Nature. Job confesses his folly and repents "in dust and ashes." The friends are then rebuked, while Job is approved and allowed to intercede on their behalf. After this he is restored to greater prosperity than ever, and becomes the father of seven sons and three daughters, as before.

INDEX

Abbreviations:—q.=quotation; r.=references, n.=note; f.=following page.

149

* G. says Downs of Surrey, but his plan on p. 322 shows the window to have been rather towards Kent.

L

COLSTONS LIMITED, PRINTERS, EDINBURGH

Lightning Source UK Ltd.
Milton Keynes UK
UKHW022136140322
400044UK00007B/1624